Resources for Women's History in Greater Manchester

by

Manchester Women's History Group

D1147595

NATIONAL MUSEUM *of* **LABOUR HISTORY**

A National Museum of Labour History Publication

First published in 1993 by the National Museum of Labour History in
association with the Manchester Women's History Group Bibliography
Project.
103 Princess Street
Manchester M1 6DD

ISBN 0 9507120 1 9

Printed by: Print Pulse (M/c)   061-223 4700

Cover: *Women tarring the road during the First World War*
              courtesy of the National Museum of Labour History

Contents

Greater Manchester

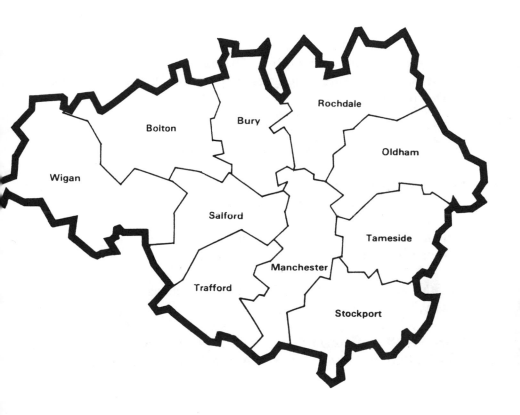

The Manchester Women's History Bibliography Project

Several people have contributed in various ways to the production of this book. When the initial group first met four years ago it consisted of Helen Drummond (who left in 1990), Amy Erickson, Dorothy Fenton, Mary Fissell, Anne Hughes, Pam Lee and Linda Walker; Stephanie Allen joined a year later. This editorial group, through regular meetings and discussion have given shape and substance to the project as it developed.

The research and compiling was undertaken principally by Linda Walker; significant contributions were made by Amy Erickson, Mary Fissell and Ann Hughes. Stephanie Allen and Pam Lee gave very useful research assistance. Ann Hughes drafted the introduction. The final editing was carried out by Ann Hughes and Linda Walker. The typesetting, layout and design were produced by Dorothy Fenton.

Notes on Contributors

Stephanie Allen is Assistant Librarian at the Liverpool Institute of Higher Education and formerly lived in Manchester.

Amy Erickson is Book Review Editor for *Gender and History* based at the University of Salford.

Dorothy Fenton is Marketing Officer at the National Museum of Labour History, Manchester.

Mary Fissell is Assistant Professor in the History of Medicine at Johns Hopkins University, Baltimore, U.S.A. and formerly lived in Manchester.

Ann Hughes is Senior Lecturer in History at the University of Manchester.

Pam Lee is a primary school teacher in Stockport.

Linda Walker is Lecturer in History at the University of Lancaster and lives in Manchester.

ACKNOWLEDGEMENTS

It would have been impossible to produce this *Guide* without the generous cooperation of all the librarians, archivists, museum and gallery curators at the institutions we have covered. All have given willingly of their time and expertise to guide us round their collections and to check the entries, often at very short notice, and in the midst of all the pressures which the difficulties of local government funding impose upon staff. We would especially like to thank the following for particular help: Kevin Mulley of Bury Archive Service and Rita Hirst of Bury Central Library; Audrey Linkman of the Documentary Photograph Archive; Catharine Rew of Manchester Jewish Museum; Sandra Martin and Ruth Shrigley of Manchester City Art Gallery and Anthea Jarvis of Platt Hall Gallery; Dr Rosalie David of Manchester Museum; Richard Bond and all his colleagues at Manchester Central Library; Dr Peter McNiven and Dr Dorothy Clayton of the John Rylands University Library of Manchester; Gaye Smith of Manchester Metropolitan University Library; Dermot Healey of Manchester Studies Tapes; Phil Dunn, and Andrew Flinn of the National Museum of Labour History; John Percy of Salford University Library; Terry Berry of Oldham Local History Library; Duncan Broady of the Police Museum; Brian Howarth of the Portico Library; Ken Howarth of the North West Sound Archive; Pam Goodman of Rochdale Local History Library and Debbie Walker of Rochdale Museum; Sue Latimer of Saddleworth Museum; Andrew Cross of Salford Archives; Tim Ashworth of Salford Local History Library, Alan Davies of Salford Mining Museum, and Judith Sandling of Salford Art Gallery; Alice Lock of Tameside Local History Library; Nancy Creamer of USDAW; Jennifer Harris of the Whitworth Art Gallery; Ruth and Edmund Frow and Alain Kahan of the Working Class Movement Library.

We are most grateful to Mike Atkinson, Sally Horrocks, Joan Mottram, Liz Stanley and Myna Trustram for sharing with us their knowledge of local sources.

We acknowledge with great thanks the generous grants awarded us by the Lipman Trust, the British Academy and the Marc Fitch Fund - without which we could not have produced such a wide-ranging volume. We thank Professor Mike Rose, Dr Jane Rendall and Jenny Kermode for supporting our grant applications. We are grateful to Manchester City Council for financial support for the launch of the *Guide*.

The group that produced the *Guide* came together through Manchester Women's History Group; the support of members of the broader Group has been essential and we thank them in particular for their useful comments when we first talked publicly about our work in November 1990. Since then we have spoken about the *Guide* at the Inaugural Conference of the National Women's History Network, in London, and at a regional meeting of the Northern Network in Lancaster. We much appreciate the useful comments we received on these occasions.

It is through the support of the National Museum of Labour History that this work is now published and we thank all those involved for their faith in us.

Figure of Autumn, Coptic c. late 4th century, courtesy of the Whitworth Art Gallery, University of Manchester.

INTRODUCTION

Manchester and the surrounding region are rich in traditions and resources for women's history. The city was at the heart of the cotton industry which provided work for several generations of women; as the home of the Pankhursts it saw the founding of the Women's Social and Political Union and was crucial in women's struggle for the vote; it is now the headquarters of the Equal Opportunities Commission. Resources for historical research are to be found in a marvellous variety of institutions, famous and obscure, publicly funded and privately maintained, large and small. Manchester's Central Reference Library is the best known of several major municipal libraries, the product of nineteenth-century civic pride and money; the academic libraries of the city contain world-renowned collections, while the recent arrival of the National Museum of Labour History with the Archives of the Labour Party has increased the area's significance as a centre for the study of British labour movements. Equally notable are the variety of smaller, more specific libraries and museums established through the dedicated work of individuals and groups. The rich collections of the Working Class Movement Library have been gathered through the heroic committed enterprise of Ruth and Edmund Frow, while Chethams Library owes its long existence to a public spirited merchant of the mid-seventeenth century. Resources reflect, to some extent at least,Manchester's history as a multi-ethnic city, constantly changing through immigration: it has a Jewish Museum, a Chinese Library Service, a Sikh Family History Project and an Irish Heritage Centre amongst many other examples.

A variety of fascinating material for the history of women is to be found in Manchester's libraries and museums but knowledge of it is in scattered hands. We began work on this guide by pooling our own information and were pleasantly surprised by what we, and other women

1

in Manchester's Women's History Group had uncovered. Many articles and books on women's history, such as *One Hand Tied Behind Us,* by Jill Liddington and Jill Norris, have used sources from Manchester. But we have learnt that women too often need to reinvent the wheel in each generation; in women's history as in women's political movements it is hard to establish traditions or to pass on what we know. Women's history is not often a priority of librarians, archivists or professional historians and women are rarely well positioned in academic institutions, or in publishing, the media, and the arts. All this contributes to a waste of expertise that we wanted to counter. Our first aim then in compiling this guide was to record and publicize what we already knew, but our project grew rapidly beyond this. We explored an ever greater variety of institutions in the Manchester region, finding a multitude of sources for women's history. We want to make knowledge of these resources as widely available as possible and to encourage further exploration of their potential.

We have tried to be as open-minded in our approach as possible although inevitably the guide reflects the expertise and pre-suppositions of the group who produced it. In the first place we have ranged as widely as we can in our search for different types of material. Historians are notoriously word-centred: most history writing, even in women's history, is based on the written word in documents, newspapers, printed books. But historians of women have been amongst the pioneers of oral history using spoken testimony to uncover the experiences and reflections of people who have not made it into the written historical record, as is often the case with women, and also to explore aspects of life such as the personal and domestic, that have not until recently been respectable subjects for historical research. Manchester Studies, a project based at Manchester Polytechnic, was an innovative Oral History and photographic retrieval enterprise; unfortunately it has now ended and its material has been dispersed to the Jewish Museum, the Documentary Photography Archive and Tameside Library. We wished to go further, however, beyond the written and spoken word, to explore the availability of visual sources such as prints, photographs, paintings and film; and of artifacts like banners and other textiles, crafts and domestic tools. Many different kinds of source can help towards understanding the myriad aspects of women's past lives.

We have tried also to be as undogmatic as possible in how we conceived of 'women's history'. The enormous wave of interest in women's history since the 1960s has inevitably prompted debate and disagreement about the nature of women's history. Should a distinction be made between a descriptive 'women's history', and a more analytic, or more politically engaged 'feminist history'? How do we balance an interest in the lives of exceptional, 'famous' women with a re-evaluation of the everyday lives of 'ordinary' women? What are the best ways of taking into account the ways in which women are divided by class, race or sexuality? Should a focus on women be replaced by an examination of 'gender' and gender relations: how men and women are defined and interrelate in changing historical situations? Or does this risk losing sight of the specific concerns of women and their oppression by men? We are aware of all these issues but have not thought it appropriate to focus on them in this guide. We have thus tried to indicate where sources exist to explore women's domestic lives, their health or their experiences of poverty but we have also noted sources concerning notable individuals - many women who were prominent and influential have not been fully discussed in a historical context. In abstract terms, the producers of this guide may have different views on women's history, and on feminism. We agree that ideally an examination of the experience of women should lead to re-assessment and to an enlarged understanding of history in general. In organising the guide, however, we have preferred to look for sources relevant to the history of women, rather than to focus on gender relationships. Potentially, any historical source may have value for an analysis of gender, but such a comprehensive survey of material in the Manchester region was beyond our resources. We have, however, become less condescending about the aim of filling in the gaps in our knowledge of women's past, as we have found out how many unexplored possibilities there are for women's history. Simply, we have tried to be as comprehensive as possible in terms of time, place, topic and type of source - inclusive rather than exclusive. However, the interests and expertise of members of the group mean that we are more at home with material on British history from 1500 rather than with earlier sources or those from further afield.

The compilers of the guide include a librarian, a museum worker, a school-teacher and four academics involved in higher education. We met through the Manchester Women's History Group which began in 1980 and has flourished ever since; it has the longest continuous existence of any women's history group in Britain. The broader group acts as a discussion and support group for women interested in women's history; its membership has fluctuated over the years but, like the bibliography project, it has never been confined to those doing 'research', still less to those who earn their living from teaching or researching history. Besides monthly meetings where a paper or other presentation is discussed, the group has stimulated a series of collective projects - joint teaching on adult education courses, production of women's history walks, research on women and Manchester between the wars, and most recently this bibliography project which has involved almost four years' work.

Our Guide covers sources **in** Manchester rather than material **about** Manchester. This is an excellent city in which to study women in ancient Egypt, as writers of seventeenth century English religious works, as nineteenth century Methodists, or as members of the Labour Party. We have tried to reflect this richness and diversity, rather than providing a manual for local women's history. Of course local museums, archives and libraries have extensive material on women in the Manchester region, while many general themes in women's history can be illuminated through local studies. (A brief list of books on women in the Manchester region is provided as an Appendix.) But it is not possible to produce comprehensive local studies without using sources from outside the region. Before the nineteenth century, Manchester was part of Lancashire for the purposes of local government, and part of the diocese of Chester for ecclesiastical affairs. The county record offices of Lancashire and Cheshire (at Preston and Chester respectively) thus have much useful material for a study of Manchester, including information on poverty, religion, crime, inheritance, as do national archives and libraries, especially the British Library and the Public Record Office in London. We have tried to indicate where local institutions hold copies of relevant material from other libraries, and the guide highlights the strengths of Manchester's libraries, museums and archives over a range of topics as well as the importance of its local collections.

We have worked institution by institution, talking to archivists and librarians, exploring catalogues and indexes. Visits were made variously by one, two, or for large collections, three or more members. Imagination and sheer luck are important in uncovering material on women, and different minds can often discover a wider range of sources and possibilities. Regular reports back and discussion meetings have refined our procedures, generated a format for entries, and greatly expanded the scope of the project. We were aware, of course, of Manchester's world famous academic and municipal libraries and of its major labour movement institutions, but we have discovered more and more   specialist museums and libraries such as the Police Museum, the Portico Library and the North West Film Archive, and have come to appreciate the importance of material held by private institutions such as Trade Unions and hospitals.

It is not possible simply to go to a library or record office and ask what they have on women; to a remarkable extent women's history popularly and in the minds of archivists still means the suffragettes. If a collection contains nothing on the struggle for the vote, the response to researchers can be discouraging. The public-private split is a shifting and contested division but the assumption that public, political affairs are firstly masculine, and secondly the most crucial subject matter for archival preservation, and historical research, is deep rooted. The suffrage campaign, a struggle for the vote - a badge of full political citizenship - is thus seen as a proper historical subject and is relatively easy to fit into conventional archival and historical categories. The problems in trying to retrieve more general sources for women's history are many-layered.

In the first place women's subordinate position in past societies means that they have directly generated fewer sources of most kinds than have men. Secondly, material produced by women is less likely to have been thought worth preserving; and finally the traditional classification schemes of most libraries, museums and record offices make it difficult to get at the sources they hold.

Until the late 19th century women have been excluded from formal power in most of the public institutions which generated the bulk of documentary material in the archives: local government, political parties, or the church; their recent role has been limited and controversial. Women have usually been less literate than men; while in many periods it was regarded as immodest for women to publish their writings and women's printed works form a tiny minority of all those published. Collections of family papers are organised around male heads of household, male family names; the prime motives for their preservation are usually to legitimate the descent of family property in the male line and to record the public activities of male M.P.s, industrialists, landowners, merchants and clerics. Deeds and land settlements were more important to preserve than the diaries or letters of women members of the family.

Archival and curatorial organising principles are not automatically friendly to women's history: collections are traditionally arranged by provenance or as types of objects, rather than on interpretive or thematic principles. The textiles in the Whitworth Art Gallery, for example, are classified by medium - 'carpets', 'embroideries' and so on, while the textiles and other artifacts in the Jewish Museum are again organised by type. For many approaches this makes sense, but it is not always convenient for those wishing to explore women's role in artistic production in particular times and places, or to discuss the place of artifacts in specific domestic settings. The Manchester City Art Gallery collection of decorative arts has an index of creators which makes it possible to highlight women silversmiths or women who worked in ceramics, but much women's art is seen as 'craft', and was produced in community settings, rather than by named individual creators who could easily be catalogued. Women's experiences in or their impact on the family are not at the forefront of archival classifications. Most library classifications have women in a subordinate position: the Dewey system which classes women next to folklore, is one of the most notorious, but also one of the most widely used. Subject indexes in particular are products of their time, and usually lag behind the interests of users. The subject index at John Rylands Library, Deansgate includes under the main heading of 'Women', the sub-headings, 'disease'; 'hygiene'; 'beauty'; as well as categories like art, industry, law, literature. Some of these we would expect in an up-to-date cataloguing system but others reveal their early 20th century origins.

Few indexes are rewarding for researchers concerned with sexuality or race: except in the Central Reference Library, 'lesbian', 'gay' or 'homosexual' are not to be found as headings, although printed books and periodicals have much to offer on sexuality while material concerning female friendship is available in many collections of family papers. The north west is a multi-racial, multi-cultural society: Rochdale, for example, has become the home of Irish, Polish, Lithuanian, Latvian, Ukrainian, Hungarian, Filipino, Indian, Pakistani, Bangladeshi and Vietnamese immigrants; Manchester has well- known Jewish, Greek, Italian, Irish, Afro-Caribbean, Asian and Chinese communities amongst others. However, the experiences and activities of these communities are still not as visible in libraries and record offices as those of the dominant white organisations; material that exists may be classified in ways not always recognised by those involved (under the heading 'West Indian', for example).

Present cataloguing systems can be frustrating, but the need to be creative and imaginative while searching through them can be part of the excitement of research: discovering the unknown or unexpected or using the familiar in a new way. Part of the adventure of doing feminist research lies in challenging the categories which highlight some aspects of women's history (suffrage or prostitution, perhaps) while sidelining or ignoring many more. For all historical researchers, luck and chance are important and the survival of material can be patchy. Business records, for example, seem more plentiful for Rochdale, Bolton and Stockport than for Salford and Trafford Park. Often traumatic changes in the local economy have not made record preservation a priority, and sadly much of the evidence of Manchester's industrial past has been lost.

If women's experiences are not necessarily taken into account when collections are defined or indexed, this emphatically does not mean that little material is available for historians of women, as we shall show below. On visiting institutions we had to work with flexibility and imagination. In smaller collections we tried to get an overview of what they held, concentrating on anything that might be relevant to women's history. We checked available lists and catalogues; looked up 'women' in subject indexes, and any other topics which seemed promising. In the Central Reference Library Archives, for example, looking up apprenticeship, cookery, diaries, poverty, prophecy, prostitution, superstition, wages, as well as more obvious subjects like 'societies' led us to very promising sources for women. In most projects (as opposed to surveys like this) you would probably start from an idea or a reference, a footnote, or bibliography in someone else's thesis, book, or article. The author might have used material in Manchester which you wanted to follow up, thinking how you could do more, or different things with the same material. Or perhaps a study of another city might encourage you to investigate if similar material was available for this area. Studies of women as Poor Law Guardians, of women and charity schools, of local women's organisations are examples.

Major libraries nearly always have extensive guides, catalogues and indexes to collections. Some libraries indeed have compiled specialist catalogues about women: the Portico Library has a list of books on women travellers; Manchester Metropolitan University (previously the Polytechnic) has a useful list of its extensive collection of women's magazines. There may be introductory guides which sketch out the major strengths of an archive or library; then alphabetical indexes to places, persons and subjects which provide brief references to collections. After that there will probably be lists or catalogues (with more description of the material) or calendars (with detailed summaries of documents) of specific collections. It is **always** worth asking the librarians or archivists for advice - they usually know the collections very well and staffing shortages often mean that there is a backlog of material which has not been listed or indexed. Librarians are usually particularly helpful if you have done some preliminary homework or searching on a topic. Of course, cutbacks in spending mean staff are often under great pressure and it is important to be understanding in the demands you make.

We have been overwhelmed by the rich material there is; how much potential exists for further work on women's history despite all that has been done over the last 20 years. It is clear, for instance, that women did have a public influence despite their formal disabilities. In some periods, the public and private were intertwined and women's religious activities were of wide significance - as Quaker and Methodist material in the John Rylands Library, for example, indicates. Great landed families, including their women members, have had an immense economic, social and political influence from medieval times. In later periods, women have often used the prevailing ideology which stressed their domestic superiority or distinctive moral influence to justify an involvement in philanthropic activities or local government. All the local libraries in this guide contain valuable material on women's participation in voluntary educational or charitable projects or their acting as Poor Law Guardians, School Board members and local Councillors. The personal lives of (mainly) elite women are illustrated in the many diaries, letters and account books found in collections of family papers. Furthermore, because great landed estates were major employers -in elaborate households, in agriculture and a variety of industrial enterprise - family collections often include fascinating material on women's employment, and on complex relationships of gender and class. The landed elite dominated local government; their papers thus often include institutional material, like manorial court rolls, or poor law records, which can be used with the records of parishes, townships, boroughs and counties, to chart the economic and social fortunes of women in local communities. For the period from the 19th century we have many records produced directly by women's social and political organisations as well as much evidence for women's lives in local government material, records of political parties or businesses.

Any attempt to order the range and variety of material in Manchester's libraries, museums, record offices and art galleries must be slightly arbitrary, but the following is offered as an attempt to indicate the range of material described in the institutional entries that follow.

1: The major academic and municipal libraries provide the standard material for any sort of historical research: secondary material - books, and current periodicals; reference tools such as biographical dictionaries; bibliographies on particular topics; abstracting services. There are guides to other libraries; for example the Equal Opportunities Commission has catalogues for the Fawcett Library in London and some major American women's history collections; the Central Reference Library and the John Rylands University Library (Main Building) have catalogues of the British Library as well as other major libraries. Major libraries also often hold copies of important material from other institutions: the John Rylands has an extensive collection of English early printed books, and suffrage material amongst its large microform holdings.

2: Major local libraries and record offices provide general sources for population, family and social structure: parish registers, rate books, census returns, local directories (often in microform).

3: There are rich holdings of books written by women, from the 17th-century Quakers in the John Rylands University Library (Deansgate Building) to the 19th-century travellers in the Portico library. Books

10

about women are very numerous indeed: local almanacs, and guides to conduct are found in many local libraries; Platt Hall has an extensive collection of etiquette books of the 18th and 19th centuries; while the important ballad compilations at Chethams and in the Central Reference Library are a good source for examining how gender relationships were presented in popular literature from the 17th century onwards. Also worth highlighting is the children's book collection held at the Didsbury site of Manchester Metropolitan University Library.

4: Newspapers and periodical publications are much used sources for women's history. Local newspapers abound, while the larger libraries hold national and inter-national titles too, along with useful indexes. The Archives of the *Guardian* are held at the John Rylands University Library. There are rich collections of periodical publications particularly in Manchester's Central Reference Library but also in the John Rylands, Bolton Local Studies Unit, The Working Class Movement Library, USDAW's library, and in the libraries of the Cooperative Union, the Equal Opportunities Commission, and the Labour Party. Women's organisations are well represented as are those of the labour, socialist and radical movements. There is a marvellous but relatively unknown collection of domestic and fashion magazines at Platt Hall.

5: Records of public bodies provide evidence for women's experiences of poverty, crime, and education as well as, for more recent times, the record of their participation and activism - as Poor Law Guardians, members of School Boards and local councils. Legal records of early manorial courts and 19th century municipal courts are held in local libraries; less predictably Manchester has a Police Museum which has some archival material. There are records of parishes and townships, of the old poor law as well as of the Victorian workhouses and the town councils. Very rich and very little used old poor law records are available for Manchester, Bolton, Salford, and Bury; the records of apprenticeship of poor girls are a useful source for women's employment in the 18th century.

The records of other institutions can be most valuable. Sometimes they have been deposited in local record offices, but it is always worth investigating whether present day businesses, political organisations, women's groups, trade unions, hospitals, newspapers, theatres and so on, have retained their own papers. We wish to highlight the following.

6: Records of local hospitals provide material on women as workers, on women's health and on women's charitable activities.

7: Religious records: the minute books of many organisations attached to local churches - women's groups, Sunday schools - offer further evidence for women's educational and charitable activities. The John Rylands Library at Deansgate holds the national records of the Methodists and important Moravian material.

8: Business records have been under-used by women's historians but often contain vital information on women's wages and working practices, managerial styles and attitudes to gender. The records of the Greg family of Styal industrial village are extensive, while the mills of Bury, Rochdale, Oldham and Bolton, and the hatters of Stockport are amongst the industries leaving interesting material.

9: Records of political organisations are well represented. Our region is especially rich in the records of the labour and socialist movements, but there is also valuable Liberal and Conservative party material. We have the Labour Party's own archives, and the major collections of the Cooperative movement in Manchester, Rochdale and Bolton. The Cooperative Union has rich Owenite material, while the Working Class

Movement Library provides information on many working class organisations. There is good Trade Union material in this library and also in local collections at Bolton, Manchester and Rochdale. The library of USDAW, which has its national headquarters in Manchester, is a valuable resource, as is the National Museum of Labour History. The records of the anti-slavery movement are well represented in the Rylands (Deansgate Building) and the Central Reference Library. Many of these bodies had women's sections, committees, associations or guilds and as our entries show, they often left minutes, correspondence and annual reports.

10: There are many records of women's own organisations although many also must have been lost, or remain hidden in the attics of daughters and granddaughters of activists. Manchester has good 'women's movement' and suffrage material: Manchester Central Reference Library holds the internationally famous papers of Millicent Garrett Fawcett as well as valuable local material. There is more at the Rylands (Deansgate) and in local libraries, including local records of the post-suffrage Women's Citizen Association, and the papers of Marjory and Sarah Lees held in Oldham Local Studies Library. Philanthropic and charitable organisations such as the Ladies Sanitary Association left fascinating records, as did consumer groups like the Electrical Association for Women (at the Museum of Science and Industry and in local collections).

11: The value of personal and family papers has been discussed already. The John Rylands (Deansgate) library is rich in family collections like that of the Leghs of Lyme; it also has extensive material concerning Elizabeth Gaskell. Manchester Central Reference Library has the papers of Shena Simon, a prominent public figure in inter-war Manchester. There are letters and diaries of a whole host of fascinating, little known or unknown women, covering many aspects of their lives, from courtship, to attendance at sermons or activity as a Poor Law Guardian.

12: Oral material provides insights into women's working lives, their health, family and political activity: the tape collections of the Jewish Museum, the Manchester Studies Unit and the North West Sound Archive are especially noteworthy.

13: Visual material like paintings, prints, photographs and film is found in many libraries as well as in art galleries and the specialist Documentary Photography Archive which includes pictures of street parties, school photographs from the 1880s, and work by women photographers. The Jewish Museum has an extensive collection of photographs covering family life, work, religion, politics, and leisure. The Northwest Film Archive provides fascinating insights into the aspirations suggested to respectable families in its collection of Co-op advertising films from 1928-45 - amongst its other gems.

14: Artifacts include costumes at the nationally important Platt Hall Gallery; trade union banners at the National Museum of Labour History and the Working Class Movement Library; the Tatton collection of 'bygones' held by the City Art Gallery with small tools like thimbles and pastry cutters along with hornbooks and dolls; ceramics and jewellery at the City Art Gallery; religious artifacts; textiles of many periods and cultures, notably the Egyptology collections at the Whitworth Art Gallery and in the Manchester Museum.

One of our pleasant discoveries was of the role women have played in the creation of the region's collections. The original John Rylands Library was founded by his widow, Enriqueta; the Egyptology collections at the Manchester Museum owe much to the energy of successive women keepers. Manchester Studies, the Documentary Photography Archive, the Equal Opportunities Commission, the Portico

Library and many others were developed by and still depend on the commitment of women librarians, archivists and curators.

This has been an exhilarating project; our imaginations have been much stimulated by the material we have found, and by our consciousness of how much there is still to do in exploring women's history. Often we have wanted to interrupt our survey in order to read the archives, study the photographs and examine the artifacts. We have been flattered and heartened by the interest and encouragement of other people, and by the welcome we have been given on our visits to institutions where hard-pressed librarians and curators went out of their way to help our searches. But we have also felt sadness and frustration at the lack of resources available to maintain and catalogue the region's collections. The dispersal of the material produced by the Manchester Studies Project is one startling example of how institutional continuity depends on financial security. Less dramatically, shortage of staff means material is not indexed or catalogued except after long delays; it is much harder to provide the extensive cross-referencing and multiple entries in catalogues which are so useful in finding material relevant to women. Opening hours are restricted by lack of funds, and financial restraints in local government and higher education have limited the acquisition of new periodicals and pruned existing titles. By contrast, the Canadian National Archives are apparently open 24 hours a day, indicating how our libraries are starved of funds.

During discussion of our project at a conference it was pointed out that old categories depend on old ideas: if what we wanted to discover could be called up easily from an entry in a card index or catalogue, it would not be novel or exciting. We want this guide to be a starting point. We have written about what we found useful and important in the institutions we visited, but others, we hope, will be stimulated into finding material we have overlooked. We have made some suggestions on using the material, but there will be many other uses we have not mentioned or thought of.

SOME PRACTICAL POINTS

The Entries

We have provided basic information about opening hours, and access; and described guides and catalogues available. We have then tried to indicate the range of material available in each institution noting examples of particular interest. Beyond that entries are not uniform in character: the variation in institutions themselves, and the collective nature of this project seemed to make uniformity undesirable. The descriptions of collections are selective rather than comprehensive, especially for the major libraries and record offices. Despite our best intentions, we have not been able to give a full account of art galleries and museums outside Manchester itself, but we have tried to indicate where further information can be obtained. Please do not assume something does not exist because we have not mentioned it. Unless otherwise stated, photocopying facilities are available in all institutions, but of course it may not be possible to obtain copies of rare or fragile books and documents. Larger institutions may offer microfilming facilities and it may be possible to obtain a microfilm print out of records preserved on microfilm (such as censuses or parish records).

Visiting Libraries, Record Offices and Museums

You should always ring or write in advance of a visit to a record office, specialist or academic library: space is often limited and seats or microform readers need to be booked; material may have to be ordered in advance (very frustrating if you are browsing, or following hunches); you may need special permission or a readers' ticket to consult rare material - bring a letter from a teacher or tutor if relevant, or some means of identification. Obviously municipal libraries are open to the public and librarians do not need notice for general enquiries; for more detailed investigations it is again worth giving advance notice. It is very important that there is advance discussion with librarians, archivists, and curators before educational or other group visits are arranged. Manuscript or rare printed material can only be used with pencils (or sometimes portable computers for the rich and technologically sophisticated.)

16

Bolton Archives and Local Studies
Central Library
Civic Centre
Le Mans Crescent
Bolton BL1 1SE
Tel: 0204 22311

Archivist: Kevin Campbell.   Local Studies Librarian: Barry Mills

Type of Institution: Public library and archives office holding local archives, newspapers, and printed material for the Metropolitan Borough of Bolton, formed in 1974 from the former county borough of Bolton, the Borough of Farnworth, and the Urban District Councils of Astley Bridge, Blackrod, Horwich, Kearsley, Little Lever, Turton (part), and Westhoughton.

Access: Open Tuesday and Thursday 9.30am - 7.30pm; Wednesday 9.30am - 1pm; Friday, Saturday 9.30am - 5 pm. Full disabled access. It is part of the Central Library/Art Gallery/Museum Complex, in the imposing building behind the Town Hall, within walking distance of the railway station and with ample public parking nearby. All welcome without advance booking; school projects should be discussed by teachers in advance of student visits. Most material is not open shelf but will be brought from the stacks by staff. The Local Studies and Archives Unit is an extremely well-organised and welcoming library.

Catalogues: There is a card index for the local studies collection covering books and pamphlets; one alphabetical sequence includes subjects, authors, titles and places. It covers some material held at Farnworth and Westhoughton libraries.
For archive material there is a very useful summary guide (a pamphlet),

17

a subject index (on yellow and white cards) and a name index (blue cards). Detailed lists of all archives are kept in files (organised by classification number) in a cupboard adjoining the card index.

A biographical index provides a guide to news cuttings and obituaries of individuals. References may be to the library's cutting collections or to a newspaper itself. Once the reference is found you should ask at the desk. Detailed subject indexes for local newspapers covering 1823 - 1894, and 1901 -1934 are kept with the archive lists.A census street index is also provided.

All the above guides and indexes are on open shelves. In addition there are available at the enquiry desk: an index to places for archives; an index to photographs and illustrations (by topic and place); a subject index to the oral history collection of tapes and transcripts; and a `Subject and Topographical News Cuttings' index covering the large collection of news cuttings compiled since 1931, again it covers topic and place.

Collections: This is a major municipal library with extensive local government and other collections, rich especially for the 19th century. There are excellent records for the local radical and socialist movements and for the women's movement.

Printed material: includes printed reports, minutes, prospectuses of many of the bodies, and societies whose records are held in Archives; local histories and theses on Bolton. Interesting items include a history of *Women's Suffrage in Bolton 1908 -1920*, compiled in 1920 by Mrs William (Mary) Haslam; prospectuses of the Bolton Women's College of Domestic Arts and Crafts which became part of the Adult Education College in 1976; and a 1976 Bolton Women's Guide produced by the local Women's Liberation Group. The library holds a full collection of the works of the Lancashire socialist novelist C. Allen Clarke who was active in the local branch of the Social Democratic Federation, and the Clarion Club. They include, *Women's Choice: a comedietta in three scenes, for three females (1894)*

Local reference material: There are microfilm copies of the census from 1841 -1891; rate books from 1897; copies of parish registers and much other useful material.

Newspapers: A good range of local papers is held including the major title *Bolton Evening News,* 1867 to date, and more ephemeral 19th century local and radical titles such as the *Bolton Free Press,* 1835 -1847 (available for consultation on microfilm). There are large collections of news cuttings and the library also holds the archive of the *Bolton Evening News* (see below).

Archives: There are rich holdings of the **local authorities and public bodies** that made up the 1974 metropolitan borough (see above) as well as for the 1974 authority itself. For Bolton itself there are very extensive records of the main council and its committees from incorporation in 1838 to 1974. Besides rate books, minutes and correspondence there are volumes of miscellaneous papers covering civic weeks, royal visits etc. There are records of the local court of Quarter Sessions from 1839 (restrictions on access to 20th century material). For Farnworth there are records of the Local Board of Health established in 1863, the Urban District Council set up in 1894 and the Municipal Borough which replaced it in 1939. Besides the usual records it is worth mentioning a Housing Survey of 1936-8 and details of unemployment schemes run in the 1920s. There is an extensive collection of official correspondence covering all aspects of local government from poor law matters to civic entertainments.

Between 1872 and 1898 there was a Bolton Rural District Sanitary Authority (from 1895 a Rural District Council) which dealt with the affairs of the rural townships and parishes around Bolton; there are minute books of its councils and committees and news cuttings. (In 1898 the areas were divided between Bolton, Westhoughton and Turton). Many records of the smaller Urban District Councils also survive, including for Horwich important material on civil defence and air raids in the second world war. There are records of Bolton Poor Law Guardians (covering an area much wider than the town) for the period

1837 -1929. Minute Books of the Guardians and their committees include material from the `Infant Life Preservation Committee'; there are also accounts, correspondence and detailed records for the workhouse. Women Poor Law Guardians in Bolton included the suffragist Mary Haslam and the socialist and Women's Cooperative Guild organiser Sarah Reddish. School Board records for Bolton and Heaton include minutes and circulars and there are many records for individual schools. The records of the townships and civil parishes from the late 17th century to the late 19th are also rich sources for women and poverty, or women's apprenticeship and employment. Most have to be consulted on microfilm. They include surveys of the poor of Bolton for 1686 -1699; cloth charity accounts for Kearsley 1707 -1792; Middle Hulton bastardy papers, 1692- 1838.

Hospital records: include extensive material on staff at Bolton General Hospital (previously Townleys Hospital) 1875 -1940, and annual reports of Bolton Royal Infirmary 1818 - 1947.

Ecclesiastical material: covers many denominations besides the established Church of England and includes microfilm copies of original registers and other records deposited at Preston or Manchester. There is material for the 19th century Swedenborgian Church and Unitarian records for the 19th and 20th centuries. Baptist material includes records of their 20th century women's organisations, while among the United Reformed material are the records of the Women's Guild of Francis Street Congregational Church, 1910 -1967. There are rich Methodist holdings including registers, minute books and Sunday School papers for individual churches.

From here we have used the Archives' own categories to make consultation of the lists easier:
Clubs, societies and trade unions: (includes political material).
Co-operative Material includes minutes for the societies at Farnworth, Kearsley, Horwich and Bolton. There are minutes and accounts of Bolton and District Cooperative Women's Guild, 1891 -1915, 1942-1964.

Labour Party Material includes the minutes of Farnworth and Worsley Constituency Labour Party, 1940 -1981 (to be consulted with the archivist's permission); election material and ward records. Miscellaneous political material includes, minutes of the Cobden Club 1865-6; records of the Tonge and Breightmet Conservative and Unionist Club; material from the General Strike Distress Committee of Little Lever; records of Little Lever Reform Club 1902 -1936.

Records of Employers and Trade Unions include: 20th century material for the Bolton Master Cotton Spinners' Association; records of Bolton and District Trades Council, 1896 -1944; National Union of Dyers, Bleachers and Textiles Workers records (which include First World War material on wartime replacement of men by women workers); and much local material mainly from the later 19th century covering NALGO (the National Association of Local Government Workers), textile unions (such as the Bolton and District Weavers and Winders Association), printing, UCATT (the Union of Construction and Allied Trades), mining and printing.

Besides the Women's Cooperative Guild material (see above) there is a separate section (ref. FW) for **women's organisations.** Material includes Minutes of the Bolton Women's Local Government Association (in which Sarah Reddish was much involved), 1897 -1918; Minutes and Annual Reports of the Bolton Women's Suffrage Association, 1908 - 1920 (with stray Women's Citizen Association minutes for 1947-8); Women's Citizen Association minutes for 1923-35, 1941-51, and annual reports and accounts; Minutes of the Bolton School for Mothers and Babies (headed again by Sarah Reddish), later the Bolton Mother and Child Welfare Association, 1908 -1953; Records of the Townswomen's Guild, 1961-1972; Minutes and case histories, correspondence, accounts of the Committee for the Reclamation of Unfortunate Women, 1867 -1870; Minutes of the committee and annual general meeting of the Bolton School Old Girls Association, 1926- 1977.

Finally this category includes the records of a variety of local groups in which women were involved: book clubs, music societies, charities, sports clubs.

Business records: these are arranged by type of concern and then individual firm. Among the `Grocers' there are the accounts of Eliza Abbott of Horwich, 1893 -1900. There are extensive records of Bleaching and other textile finishing industries; coalmining (especially the Ladyshore Coal and Terra Cotta Company); cotton textiles and engineering. The records of New Eagley (cotton) mills include material on child employment in the 1880s, and wage books and other material exist for research into women's work. The records of the Bolton Evening News include, besides wage books and other day-to-day business records, correspondence with authors whose books were published in the paper in serial form, and material concerning the General Strike.

Family and estate papers: (n.b. often include business records and many include photographs). The Crompton papers include the personal and business accounts of Samuel Crompton (of spinning mule fame); family correspondence, including that of women members from the 18th to the 20th centuries; and material on the Swedenborgian church in which the family were active, 1804 -1853.

The papers of the **Haslam** family of Bolton include material on the family firm, John Haslam and Co., and interesting material on the suffragist and Poor Law Guardian Mary Haslam. There are travel diaries of Mary and her husband in Europe, 1896-1920; autobiographical sketches, and her diary as a Poor Law Guardian 1893-1904. Mary Haslam was a member of the Heywood family of Bolton; their family papers include an 1844 survey of the age, sex and literacy of employees of cotton mills in Manchester and District.

The Alice Foley Collection is the papers of the author of *A Bolton Childhood* (Manchester University Extra Mural Department, 1973).

Alice Foley (1891 -1974) was a trade unionist, feminist, and J.P. She was active in Bolton Women's Citizen Association, Bolton Socialist Club and Sunday School and so on, and worked as secretary to the Bolton Weavers and Winders Association from 1949. The collection consists of 39 items, mostly drafts and copies of speeches, articles and essays. They include a 1930 item, `The Cotton Dispute: the Woman Weaver's Point of View'. There are also photographs.

Other small collections covering individual women include the correspondence and nursing records of Marion Hindle of Bolton, 1900 -1980 (restricted access); papers of Edith Norris of Bolton, genealogist and stained glass designer (permission needed); autobiography and photographs of Hilda Snowmen of Adlington and Bolton, b. 1901, concerning her employment as a half-timer in the mill, and her marriage.

Oral history material: there is a large collection of tapes produced by the Bolton Oral History Project of the early 1980s, and copies of Manchester Studies material relevant to Bolton. Most have transcripts and, for women, they cover such themes as childbirth, work, home life and so on. The Bolton Oral History Project produced a resource pack, `Growing up in Bolton' which includes photographs and cassettes. It has recently been reprinted by Bolton Environmental Education Project and is available, along with much other local history material, from the shop at the Central Library.

Photographs and illustrations: a large collection covering many local topics. Many family collections include photographs, while the Bolton Library Handbill Collection covers local elections, celebrations and the like, mostly of the mid 19th century. This is listed in the Archives lists under the reference ZZ130.

Bury Archive Service
1st Floor Derby Hall Annexe, Edwin St (off Crompton St)
Bury BL9 0AS
Tel: 061 797 6697
Archivist: Kevin Mulley

Type of institution: Public archive holding local authority and other material from the boroughs of Bury, Prestwich, Radcliffe, Ramsbottom, Tottington and Whitefield, amalgamated to form Bury Metropolitan Borough in 1974. The collection consists primarily of 19th and 20th century local government records, family and business papers, and church, political, trade union and local society records.

Access: Open Tuesdays 10am - 1pm and 2 -5 pm; other weekdays (and possibly the first Saturday morning in the month) by appointment only. No disabled access, but contact the archivist for alternative arrangements. As access to the archive is difficult, it is advisable to use the town car parks and walk to the archive which is near the market place. All researchers welcome, but GCSE and A-level teachers are encouraged to discuss projects with the archivist in advance of student visits. Bring a record office ticket if you have one, or identification if you do not. Photocopying available.

Catalogue: Each archive group (that is, all records produced or retained by a single organisation or individual) has a draft descriptive list (currently being typed). There is no general index to the lists, but indexes are available for certain archive series.

Collections: n.b. The archive is not yet licenced under the Public Records Act, so many local public records are held in GMC Record Office, including magistrates' court records, 1930s clerks' notes of evidence with much social detail, bastardy orders and coroners' records. New Poor Law Union records for Bury are held in the Lancashire Record Office at Preston.

Local government records include those for borough and district councils, plus predecessor authorities such as local boards of health, civil parishes and improvement commissioners. Examples are: Bury and Pilkington township poor law records, c.1675-c.1850 (affiliation orders, workhouse accounts, etc); rate books for Bury and Pilkington from the late 18th century, and for most other areas from the late 19th century; council/local board/committee (Education Committee, Pension Committee, etc) minute books from the mid 19th century for most areas, with some gaps; school records from the 1870s; town clerks' correspondence especially from World War I onwards, covering all aspects of council business, including records of evacuees, billeting, women employed by the council and local authority funds to help the families of servicemen.

Personal papers include the preaching notes and a biographical sketch of local methodist preacher Florence Howarth (1904-70), and the personal reminiscences of Mrs Gittins (1920s-30s).

Family and business papers: Bealey of Radcliffe, 1818-1919: Mary Bealey (d.1858) ran the family bleachworks from 1821 to 1850 after her husband died. This prominent Methodist family founded the Radcliffe Close Chapel and School (1838-1931) and the Bealey Memorial Convalescent Hospital (1903-36).

Woodcock & Sons, solicitors, 1780-1946: papers include the deeds of Lord Derby's estate from 1870; several generations of personal papers, containing the letters of Samuel and Jane Woodcock about domestic matters (1832-58) including local comment on their childlessness, and a sister's involvement with a Catholic priest.

Hutchinson of Bury and Prestwich, 1727-1950: deeds, letters, diaries, photos, correspondence (1827-91), 19th century recipe books; financial papers for the estates of Mary Joanna (d.1887) and Sarah (d.1888), and their sketch books, poetry and autographs. There are also the records of W. & J. Hutchinson Ltd, cotton manufacturers (1863-1926), and correspondence of Mrs H. Hutchinson about her son missing in action in World War I.

Bury Savings Bank (now Trustee Savings Bank), 1822-1972: account information, including occupations, on individual depositors and on societies, like the Female Friendly Sick Society in the 1820s.

Thomas Robinson & Co., bleachers: wage books (1907-33).
Robert Battersby & Sons, woollen manufacturers, 1728-1878: accounts for outworkers include some women.

There is an extensive collection of nonconformist **church records,** particularly Methodist, including registers of births, marriages, deaths and burials; Stand Lane Congregational Church School records from 1816; trustees' minutes; class leaders' minutes; funds for missionary societies; social events; pew rents; choir registers; sunday school and temperance society records; and minutes of teachers' meetings and preachers' meetings.

Political records include the Bury and Radcliffe Labour Party from 1948 and the Bury North Liberal Association, 1970s (permission needed). There is material on women councillors among council and party records, but no personal papers. See reports in the *Bury Times* and other local papers which covered council meetings.

Trade union records include the Bury Operative Cotton Spinners Association (1882-1967) and the AUEW Bury District (1920-48).

Society records include the Bury (cotton famine) Relief Committee (1862-74) with a 'workfare' scheme for women unemployed because of the American civil war, giving details of family incomes, etc; Prestwich and District Nursing Association (1912-53); League of Nations Union/ UN Association (1920-82); Bury Cooperative Society (1858 onwards); Ramsbottom Industrial and Providential Society Ltd (1862-1968) wage books, members' and share ledgers; Prestwich Cricket, Tennis & Bowling Club (1900-74); and the Bury Music Circle (20th century).

Photographs are scattered among the archive groups -- e.g., family albums of the 19th and 20th centuries in the Hutchinson papers; slum property in Ramsbottom in the 1930s; and May Day and Whit walks of Stand Church. See also the photographic collection at Bury Local History Library.

Contact the archivist for details of numerous smaller family, business, trade union and local society archive collections.

Bury Central Library
Textile Hall
Manchester Road
Bury BL9 0DR
Tel: 061 705 5871
Librarian: Rita Hirst

Type of Institution: Public library built in 1901 as part of a joint art gallery and library complex. It covers the boroughs of Bury, Prestwich, Radcliffe, Tottington and Whitefield which were amalgamated to form Bury Metropolitan Borough in 1974, as well as the ancient parish and old Rural District of Bury. The library combines reference, lending and local history sections. It has a good range of local history material, much of it pre-19th century, reflecting Bury's importance as a pre-industrial market town which became a centre for the textile trade. It has printed and archive material relating to local government, local firms, societies, families, individuals, churches and schools, as well as extensive collections of pamphlets, newscuttings and photographs.

Access: Hours are Monday, Tuesday, Thursday, Friday 10am - 5.30pm; Wednesday 10.00 am - 7pm; Saturday 10am - 4.30pm. Photocopying available. Disabled access. The library is one block from the bus and metro station.

Catalogue: There is a separate local history collection card catalogue arranged by author, class and subject; a surname catalogue of local Bury families, and separate indexes for newscuttings, pamphlets and photographs. The local history librarian, Rita Hirst, has compiled an extremely useful and detailed subject index called *Bury and Adjacent Places, 1752-1783* which lists items taken mainly from the *Manchester Mercury*; examples of subject entries are: crime - rape; bawdy house - keeping of; marriages - breach of promise; wives - runaway. The index is available at the service counter.

Collections: Local history material includes council minutes; local newspapers such as the *Bury Times* (1855-) Manchester Mercury (on microfilm, 1752-1830); a variety of directories: general, street, trade, professional and commercial - for example, *Bury Directory* (1814-15) contains classified lists of trades and professions; a manuscript record of local events and general occurrences (1752-1876) compiled by John Shaw; items about Bury Market. The library also holds photocopies of records relating to Bury and its environs held in other record offices and libraries. For example, it has transcripts from the Derby Muniments held at the Lancashire Record Office (Lord Derby was the major landowner in Bury) which include a survey of Bury, 1701, and other miscellaneous items which have been extracted from the Records by Norman Tyson. Legal records include a Report of the Bury Watch Committee (1893) and miscellaneous items such as an appeal for charity on behalf of John and Mary Grimes, wrongly convicted of highway robbery (1830). Political records exist for the Conservative Party, *History and Handbook of the Bury Unionist Bazaar* (1912) and Bury Socialist Society (1904).

The following are items of particular interest.

Poor Law records: There are some records for Tottington Lower End on microfilm. These include a very interesting census of the poor taken in 1817. They also include apprenticeship papers and bastardy orders. Records of Bury New Poor Law Union include indentures made out by overseers of the poor - for example, for Ann Buckley, a poor girl from Bury who was apprenticed as a servant to a tailor in Bolton in 1733. Most of the Poor Law records for Bury are in Bury Archives.

School records: There are numerous records for local schools such as Bank Street Girls' School (1885), the Convent Grammar School, Bury (1878-1978), Bury Grammar School for Girls and Bury High School (both 20th century). Also of interest are records for local charity, industrial, ragged and local authority schools from the late 19th century.

Ecclesiastical records exist for local sunday schools and a number of churches and chapels: Congregationalist, United Reform, Primitive Methodist, Presbyterian, Unitarian, the Society of Friends, Church of England and Methodist (with a list compiled for all Methodist chapels in the Bury area).

Business, employment and trade union records: Bury was a centre for textiles, papermaking and leatherworking amongst other industries, and there are many records for local firms of which the following are a selection: accounts and wages books; labour certificates, birth certificates and other records for half timers and apprentices; posters, photographs and newscuttings such as an item about Catherine Horne who started work at the age of six in a local textile mill, and at the time of the interview in 1911 was Ramsbottom's oldest female resident. Published histories include an article by Frances Collier about workers at the firm of Peel and Yates, Calico Printers, *The Family Economy of the Working Class in the Cotton Industry 1784-1833*, Chetham Society Publication, 1965. Trade union records include the annual reports of Bury Trades and Labour Council (1903-21, incomplete), andBury Trades Council Annual Reports (1947-66).

Society records: There are records for the Bury and District Cooperative Society, and an unpublished typescript (with photographs) by Anne Kirkham 'A Short History of the Women's Co-operative Guild, Bury Branch' (c. 1940). Other items of interest are Annual Reports (1905-43, incomplete) of the Charity Organisation Society, Bury, which continued as the Bury Family Welfare Association (Annual Reports for 1947-69); Rules to be observed by members of Bury Women's Sick List (benevolent society) (1837); Rules of the Bury Ladies' Charity (1887). See also F. Howarth, 'The Female Union Society, Holcombe Brook' in *Lancashire* vol.3, 3 November 1982.

Personal and family papers: Personal items include a newscutting about Nellie Halstead, an Olympic runner before the second world war, a magazine article about Jenny Burgoyne and life in a Lancashire hostelry, a letter from Mary Brown, a debtor in Lancaster Castle to William Holt of Ramsbottom (1814), and transcripts of wills made by local women. Of particular interest is material relating to the Hoyle family, woollen manufacturers of Bury: Annie Hoyle's Scribbling Diary for 1898 contains rich detail about her life, her family and friends; there is a biography of *Rachel Hoyle* (1901) and an autobiographical typescript 'My Life's Work' (1968) by Edith Sharples (also of the Hoyle family) who became one of the first policewomen. The library has a copy of deeds of dower, marriage and settlement between Sir John Pilkington and Elizabeth Trafford, with a list of tenants of the family's Bury estates in 1435; the originals are in Chetham Library. Also of interest is *Hell's Foundations* by Geoffrey Moorhouse, 1992 - a study of the effect of Gallipoli on the town of Bury, including the effects on the women who were left behind and the struggles of the widows and children in the years after the war. The author acknowledges the help of Alice Mitchell whose mother, Alice Scrowcroft, was left with two young children to bring up.

Chetham's Library
Long Millgate, Manchester M3 1SB
Tel. 061 834 7961
Librarian: Michael Powell. Assistant: Jackie Stanton

Type of Institution: Privately funded public library, established mid-1650s and open to the public ever since. Located inside Chetham's School. Good collection of printed works, especially in local history. Also collections of muniments (manuscripts and personal collections), photographs and engravings, and broadside ballads.

Access: Open Monday to Friday 9.30am - 12.30pm and 1.30pm - 4.30pm. Books fetched at any time, but telephone ahead for muniments. Disabled access is limited; telephone for information.

Catalogue: Secondary works indexed by author/title and by subject, including headings like 'Education - women', 'Lancs - biography', 'Suffrage', 'Witchcraft', and 'Women'. Muniments collection has a handlist, plus a subject/name card index with entries like:
Alehouses. Rules for keeping (1658); Allon, Susanna, of Barnsley, Yorks. (1752); Apprenticeship records; Audley, Elizabeth, cousin of Ann Hinde (1724).

Collection: The muniments collection includes the following types of records, with examples of items useful for women's history:
Medieval manuscripts - Latin manuscripts on wifely conduct; French, Dutch and English books of hours and prayers; medical treatises (all 15th century); earlier saints' lives.
Private family papers - journals, letters, deeds, recipes, etc.; 17th century and 18th century commonplace books and household books (one German set and many English); 16th century Cholmondeley family tenures; 16th century medical recipes.
Printed items: local history collections, including 17th century and 18th century histories of Manchester and a collection of Yorkshire epitaphs; sermons; 18th century Italian medical book.

Institutional records: 17th century hospital account book and Lanca-shire books of rates; 18th century accounts of Overseers of the Poor.

The photographs are mostly of buildings; many are glass slides from the turn of the century. There is an (incomplete) card index of engravings contained in the library's 17th century, 18th century and 19th century books. One 1717 volume, for example, contains more than 150 prints of plants and insects by the celebrated German engraver Maria Sibilla Merian.

The Halliwell-Phillips Collection of Broadsides, Ballads and Proclama-tions contains 3100 items, most of which date from the late 17th century and 18th century. It is indexed by subject.

Engraving of Maria Sibilla Merian, c. 18th Century, courtesy of Chetham's Library.

The Co-operative Union Library
Holyoake House, Hanover Street
Manchester M60 0AS
Tel: 061 832 4300
Librarian: Roy Garratt

Type of Institution: Private library attached to the national headquarters of the Co-operative Union in Manchester. It holds selected records of the co-operative movement, including the Women's Co-operative Guild, and has a small but good library of books on trade union and labour movement history, and social and economic conditions in Britain in the nineteenth and twentieth centuries.

Access: Hours are Monday to Friday 10am - 4.45pm. The library primarily serves staff of the Co-operative Union, but scholars, students and research workers are also welcome. Disabled access: two shallow steps at the entrance to the building; the library is on the ground floor. Photocopying facilities are available.

Catalogue: Researchers using the archive collections are advised to consult the library staff. There is a card index for the book library, and a bibliographical guide compiled by Jean Gaffin and Rosamund Hollingsworth, which lists the major WCG collections in the LSE Library and the Brynmor Jones Library at Hull University.

Women's Co-operative Guild records:
Photocopies of the papers of Mary Lawrenson (1883-1906), one of the founders of the Guild.
Woman's Outlook, complete set, 1919-1967.
Head Office Monthly Bulletin, 1947-1962.
Annual Reports - from the 10th report (1892-3) up to the present day with a few missing.
Resolutions and Amendments to the WCG Congress from 1921.

Pamphlet collection: This is an extensive collection dating from 1897 and is an excellent source for the Guild's radical interests and campaigns.

Women's Co-operative Guild Newsletter - 1970s, 1980s.

Miscellaneous publications, e.g. WCG Handbook, c.1956.

The International Co-operative Women's Guild, Reports and Pamphlets, 1940s, 1950s;

The International Woman Co-operator, 1946-1960.

Irish Co-operative Women's Guild, Annual Reports, 1913 - 1973, but many years missing.

Scottish Co-operative Women's Guild, Annual Reports, 1904-1971, but many years missing.

Related Co-operative Society material: Manuscript Collections of Robert Owen and G. J. Holyoake Papers.

Printed books include: Margaret Llewelyn Davies, *The Women's Co-operative Guild,* 1904. Catherine Webb, *The Woman with the Basket. The Story of the Women's Co-operative Guild,* 1927. A. Buchan, *History of the Scottish Co-operative Women's Guild, 1892-1913,* 1913. K.M. Callen, *History of the Scottish Co-operative Women's Guild, Diamond Jubilee 1892-1952.* Emmy Freundlich, *Housewives Build a New World,* 1936. *Of Whole Heart Cometh Hope. Centenary Memories of the Co-operative Women's Guild,* 1983. Iris Webb, *People Who Care. A Report on Carer Provision in England and Wales for the Co-operative Women's Guild,* 1987.

The library holds copies of **theses** on the WCG including: Gillian Scott, 'The Politics of the Women's Co-operative Guild: Working Women and Feminism During the First World War', unpublished MA Thesis, Sussex University, 1981.

Documentary Photography Archive
c/o Cavendish Building
Cavendish Street
Manchester
M15 6BG
Tel: 061 247 1765
Curator: Audrey Linkman

Type of Institution: The archive is an independent educational charity which was established in 1985. It seeks to create and preserve a photographic record of the North West. The archive combines an historical collection of some 80,000 items copied from the family "albums" of local people with a growing body of contemporary commissioned material. The DPA undertakes research into the social history of photography, and is concerned to develop effective systems for the archiving of the visual image. Emphasis is placed on the documentation of the photograph - partly as a way of encouraging the social historian to make better use of the visual image in written history. The historical archive, in particular, is a rich source of material for women's history because of its focus on the family, and the DPA's concern to chart mundane, ordinary aspects of life.

Access: Open to the public. The collection is housed at the GMC Record Office, 56 Marshall Street, New Cross, Manchester, M4 5FU and can be viewed there on Tuesdays 10 am - 1 pm, 2 pm - 4.30 pm. It is possible to see material at other times by appointment. Contact Audrey Linkman at the Cavendish Building address. She can assist with preliminary enquiries. Disabled access: prior notice required. Where commercial enquirers cannot visit in person, a search fee (minimum £30) will be levied. Copy prints can be purchased.

Catalogue: The Archive of Family Photographs is filed both in family sequence and in subject order. The images are supported by detailed contextual information about the family, subject content of each photograph and relevant information about its manner of production. This is essentially a collection of 35mm copy negatives accessed via contact prints. The DPA produces information leaflets about its work and the collections.

Collections:
The Archive of Family Photographs: This records the period c.1880 - 1940 and in geographical terms covers the cotton towns of North East Lancashire, the Cheshire border and North Derbyshire. The collection is strongest on people and their daily activities. It reflects the treatment and themes which attracted both professional and amateur photographers. Work, particularly in the cotton industry, leisure, school and domestic interiors are subjects which are well represented. Other themes are marriage, entertainment, voluntary, political and trade union activity, religion, temperance, war work. The archive also contains copies of early daguerreotypes. Particular subject items which have reference to women: British Women's Committee against War and Fascism; Church Girls' Brigade, family planning, may and rose queens, midwifery, Mothers' Unions, nursing, dressmaking, tailoring, needlework, Jewish Board of Guardians, office workers, prostitution, domestic service, suffrage, convents, YMCA, Women's Royal Air Force, Women's Royal Voluntary Service.

Contemporary commissions: Each commission comprises negatives, contacts, work prints, written records and (in some cases) exhibition prints, together totalling some 15,000 items. Projects include Martin Parr on Shopping in Salford (1985), Shirley Baker on Manchester Airport (1987), Clement Cooper on Youth in Moss Side (1987), Tom Wood on Care in the Community (1990). Each commission has its individual catalogue.

Deposits: The archive includes an assortment of original material comprising family photographs, amateur collections, postcards, albums, lantern slides, etc. The DPA houses the collections of Open Eye Gallery, Liverpool, and the Lancashire and Cheshire Photographic Union.

Equal Opportunities Commission Information Centre
Overseas House, Quay Street
Manchester M3 3HN
Tel: 061 833 9244
Librarian: Pat Darter

Type of Institution: The information centre is run by the EOC for its own staff and for the public.

Access: Open Monday to Friday, 9am - 5pm to anyone. You will have to tell the security man on the desk at the front door of the building that you wish to visit the EOC Information Centre on the 4th floor. The Centre gives you a card to show at the front door desk on subsequent visits, and which enables you to check out material. For group visits, please contact the librarian in advance.
Disabled access: ramp to entrance and lifts to 4th floor.

Catalogue: A computerised catalogue for books and journal articles. Press cuttings are arranged by subject in files. The staff are very helpful, so always ask if you can't find something.

Collection: Excellent collection of some 350 current periodicals - mostly British, but also international - on open shelves for browsing. Those dealing specifically with women include *African Woman, Asian Woman, Association of Radical Midwives, Feminist Arts News, Feminist Issues, Feminist Review, Feminist Studies, Gender & Society, Gender & Education, Hecate, History Workshop Journal, Hypatia, Journal of Law and Society, Journal of Marriage and the Family, Manushi, Ms. Magazine, National Women's Register, New Literature on Women, Resources for Feminist Research, Sex Roles, Signs, Trouble & Strife, The Woman Engineer, Women's Studies Abstracts, Women's Studies International Forum.* Plus many other trade union, professional, labour, and employment newsletters and law periodicals. Discontinued periodicals - like 1970s feminist magazines *Red Rag* and *Shrew* - are kept separately and must be requested at the desk.

The book collection is mostly concerned with gender issues, but it is eclectic, including a fair amount of sociology, but little history. There are also assorted pamphlets, and multitudinous government publications -- Statistical Reports of the EOC on women's and men's relative position in education, employment, wealth, etc, plus reports of the International Labour Organisation, the European Community, and other governmental bodies. There is a collection of posters, postcards, and badges of the feminist movement since the 1970s, and records of music by women composers and performers. Books and records are available for loan.

Good collection of current reference material, including Bibliofem, which lists the catalogue of the Fawcett Library in London (out-of-date but still helpful), the catalogues of the Radcliffe College and Smith College archives in the United States, and assorted grants directories.

General, Municipal, Boilermakers and Allied Trades Union (GMB)
Residential College, College Road,
Whalley Range, Manchester M16
Tel: 061 861 8788
Contact: Peter Carter: Education Manager.

Type of Institution: Residential college and conference centre owned by the GMB.

Access: Open to all bona-fide researchers on application to the Director in normal office hours. Good disabled access.

Collections: The major archives of the GMB have been deposited in the Working Class Movement Library (see separate entry) but the College still has material relating to the Association of Women Clerks and Secretaries: minutes, correspondence, press cuttings, journals, and annual reports from the early 20th century to 1940 when the Association became part of the Clerical and Administrative Union, and ultimately part of the GMB

Greater Manchester County Record Office
56 Marshall Street
New Cross
Manchester
M5 5FU
Tel: 061 832-5284
County Archivist: Maureen Patch

Type of Institution: Public archive which contains records pertaining to the County of Greater Manchester. Deposits include public records such as courts of quarter sessions, coroners' courts, hospital records and Charity Commissioners accounts, official records of the GM County Council, family and estate papers, business and commercial records, trade unions, societies and organisations.

Access: Opening hours are Monday 1 - 5 pm; Tuesday - Friday, 9am - 5pm, and on the 2nd and 4th Saturday of each month 9am - 4pm. Disabled access is difficult with a short flight of stairs up or down to the lift. Public records are deposited under the relevant sections of the Public Records Acts (1958 and 1967) and are therefore closed for a minimum of 30 years up to 100 years, e.g. clinical information. Researchers are asked to consult the County Archivist before making a visit to consult Public Records.

Catalogue: The catalogue is arranged according to standard record office procedures with documents listed according to provenance. GMCRO has its own booklet: *Summary Guide to Collections*, £3.95.

Collections: There are records for various hospitals in the Greater Manchester area, some of which are twentieth century, while others for the Florence Nightingale Hospital, Bury General and Fairfield General go back to the Victorian period. Public records (for access see above).

Personal and family papers: These include microfilmed copies of the Indexes of births, marriages and deaths from the General Registry Office, St Catherine's House, (1837-1927). Probate records: grants of wills and letters of administration (1858-1941). Marriage registers from methodist chapels in Bury and Rochdale (1890-1983). Family and Estate papers: e.g. Howarth Family of Tottingham (1547-1923); Barrow family of Lancaster; Wadkin and King Families of Manchester (Quakers) (1682-1909); Assheton Family of Middleton (1197-1837) (personal papers of Lady Anne); Egerton Family, Earls of Wilton (Heaton Hall); Entwistle Family of Foxholes (nr. Rochdale).

Business, employment and trade union records: Company records: e.g. Bury Cooper and Whitehead - records of the Royal George Mills, Oldham (1728-1980); Milnrow Spinning Co - records 1907-78, including wages books. Trade union records: National Union of Textile and Allied Workers (1867-1975); National Union of General and Municipal Workers, Rochdale and Castleton branches (1906-66). Journals of the textile industry: including *Textile Weekly, The Textile Manufacturer*. Trade Directories: e.g. Raffald's (1772), White's (1847, 1853).

Education Records include those for Charter Street Ragged School (1861-1967).

Newspapers: *The Manchester Guardian* (1821-1967); *The Daily Dispatch* (1900-55); *Manchester Evening News* (1872-1970); *The Manchester Evening Chronicle* (1897-1963); *The Rochdale Recorder* (Feb-Dec 1827); *The Stockport Advertiser* (Feb-Dec 1887).

Greater Manchester Police Museum
Newton Street
Manchester M1 1ES
Tel: 061 856 3287
Curator: Duncan Broady

Type of Institution: Private museum containing material on local police forces in the Greater Manchester area, and records relating to public order, registered aliens, and crime. There is much of interest to social historians and to researchers working on women, young people, and immigrant communities. The collection consists of photographic and documentary material, mostly late 19th and 20th centuries.

Access: All researchers welcome, including GCSE students doing project work. Monday to Friday, 9am - 4.30pm by appointment. Disabled access is difficult, but can be arranged with prior notification. Photocopying facilities.

Catalogue: No catalogue as such, but museum staff will help with enquiries and provide detailed information about collections. There is a useful *Guide to the Archives of the Police Forces of England and Wales* by Ian Bridgeman and Clive Emsley, published by the Police History Society.

Archival material: Aliens' Registers from World War I to c. 1950, deposited by the Police Registration District of Salford give census-type information; there is restricted access. Police General Orders include permission given to groups and organizations (e.g. WSPU, NUWSS) to hold demonstrations and sell newspapers, as well as arrangements for the protection of public buildings from attack by suffragettes. Material in the Watch Committee minutes 1896-1974 covers similar ground to General Orders; organisations mentioned include Manchester and Salford Women's Trades and Labour Council, North of England Society for

Women's Suffrage, WSPU. Orders to Superintendents from the Chief Constable's Office to the Manchester Police include notes and memos about "known" suffragettes who might commit acts of civil and criminal disobedience. For World War II there are ration books, identity cards, leaflets. Thieves Books are records of men and women convicted of crimes, indicating offence, sentence, and details of individual criminals; they include photographs and are mostly late 19th, early 20th century. Also of interest are *Modus Operandi* books which are detective picture books of suspects.

There are records of women in the police force, mainly local, including the personal papers of Clara Walkden, one of the earliest policewomen in Manchester (1921-43); records of Nellie Bohanna, member of the Women's Auxiliary Police Force (1941-72), who became Policewoman Superintendent in Manchester; records relating to the first conference of provincial policewomen, (1937).

Records of the Manchester City Policewomen Department include details of undercover work in local clubs, eg., the Beat Club, giving very useful information on the social history and leisure of young people in the 1950s and 1960s. The records note details of underage girls and infringements of licensing laws.

Printed material includes the *Policewomen's Review* (1937 only), *Police Review* and *Police Magazine* which has occasional historical articles, e.g. on Mary Allen, a suffragette turned policewoman c. 1919-1921.

Photographic collection: This is documented and catalogued. Subjects include suffrage campaigns, policewomen, women mill workers on strike.

Manchester Central Library
St Peter's Square, M2 5PD
Tel: 061 234 1986

Type of Institution: Public library covering all subject areas in the arts, social sciences, medicine, science and technology. The library opened on its present site in 1934 and its circular building of Portland stone is a distinctive landmark in the city. Its predecessor, the first rate-supported public library in the United Kingdom, established in 1852, was housed in the Hall of Science in Campfield, the home of the Owenite socialist movement.

Access: Reference facilities are available to all, with borrowing rights for those who can provide two proofs of address. There is full disabled access to virtually all parts of the building (the upper floor of the Language and Literature Library is, unfortunately, still inaccessible). A specialist unit serves visually impaired people. The function of this 'VIP' Unit is to allow visually impaired people to gain access to the full range of library stock and services through such means as the Kurzweil Reading Machine, computers, brailling and large print transcription services. This is open the same hours as the rest of the library except for Friday evenings and staff are extremely helpful.

Hours of opening, except where stated, are as follows: Monday, Tuesday, Wednesday, Friday: 10am - 8pm; Thursday, closed; Saturday 10am - 12 noon, 1pm - 5pm. For access to rare books, archives and other unique material (items whose classification number begins 'BR' or 'ms') you need to complete a 'Book Rarity Form' in the library; the library posts it to you and you bring it in; or you can phone the relevant library and ask for the form to be posted in advance. This is not necessary where material is to be consulted under close supervision in the Archives. Some places in term time are available in the St Peter's Children's Centre, Town Hall Extension, next to the library, for parents using the library. For further information ring 061 234 3246.

Catalogue: A main card catalogue for all the library's stock is housed in the catalogue hall on the first floor; it is arranged by name and classification, with a subject index to the classification numbers. In addition each department has its own lending catalogue and fiver departments (Arts, Music, Language and Literature, Chinese and Local Studies) also have reference catalogues for their own material. The cards in this main catalogue do not indicate to which department items belong, but this can be worked out from the Dewey classification number. Local Studies has relevant material in all classifications. The material listed under Manchester (with numerous sub-headings) is a very useful starting point for local researchers. There are a few bibliographical guides in the catalogue hall: British National Bibliography and Whitaker's Cumulative Book List are on open shelf while Whitaker's ISBN list, *British Books in Print, American Books in Print,* and *Books in English* are on microfiche. The National Union and British Library catalogues are in Book Services on the third floor and can be consulted on request at any first floor enquiry counter, up to 4pm on weekdays.

Arts Library: 061 234 1974

Catalogue: There are separate reference and lending card catalogues organised by name and classification, with an index to subjects.

Collections: The reference collection includes books, periodicals, microforms on all aspects of the Fine, Decorative and Performing Arts, plus sport and leisure. The smaller, lending collection includes books and slides.

There are useful general abstracts, indexes and bibliographies such as *Art Index*, and *Design and Applied Arts Index*, plus specialised bibliographies and dictionaries of women artists and designers (e.g. Donna Bachmann and Sherry Piland, *Women Artists: an historical, contemporary and feminist bibliography)*. The library subscribes to the 'Women

Artists Slide Library' and has also purchased a set of microfiches on 'Contemporary Women Artists in the W.A.S.L.'. The subject catalogue offers a wide variety of topics under the heading 'women', including artists, portraits, costume, and the less obvious Film Noir, Irish painting. There are details of exhibitions by the Manchester Society of Women Painters, 1880 -83; and material on the Attic Club, a society of women artists active in Manchester in the 1920s and 1930s.

Special collections include fashion photographs from the News Chronicle c. 1890 -1960; Annie Horniman material in the Local Theatre Collection, consisting of biographies and other books, newscuttings, photographs, and letters concerning the pioneering theatrical manager. The library also holds a microfiche copy of the Horniman collection in the John Rylands University Library of Manchester.

Watson Music Library: 061 234 1976

Catalogue: separate card catalogues organised by subject, author and classification for the reference and the lending stock. There are a variety of subject indexes, organised by type of music or score: music rarities; subjects before 1800; subjects after 1800. This last section includes a few works by women, such as May Hanna Brahe, 'As I went a-roaming', lyrics by Helen Taylor. There are also indexes to Songs, Chamber Music, Full and Miniature scores.

Collections: books, periodicals, music scores. Besides good general bibliographical and other reference material useful to those interested in women and music, there is a comprehensive collection of biographical material on women musicians. Most useful material is classified at 780.17 (women in music); 780.81 (bibliographies); 927.8 (autobiographies/biographies). The library takes the annual *Music Index* and periodicals include *British Journal of Music Education; Folk Roots; Classical Music; Music Review*. General works on women musicians include Charles E. Claghorn, *Women Composers and Hymnists: a* *concise biographical dictionary* (1984); Jane Weiner Lepage, *Women Composers, Conductors and Musicians of the Twentieth Century: selected biographies* (1980); Joan Skowronski, *Women in American music: a bibliography* (1978). There are biographies or autobiographies of women folk singers, jazz musicians and popular musicians as well as classical singers and musicians; they include Clara Butt, Maria Callas, Ira Haendel, Jacqueline du Pre, Bessie Smith, Joan Baez, Billie Holiday and Barbara Streisand.

Language and Literature Library: 061 234 1972

Located on the fourth floor, primarily for students and researchers, it contains an extensive stock of British and non-British literature, including books in languages other than English, periodicals and works of criticism. There are also tapes and Special Collections of rare books and manuscripts. There is loan material, open shelf reference material and stored reference works (the bulk of the collection) for which request slips must be filled in.

Catalogue: There is a catalogue for the lending collection and a card catalogue arranged by author/title/and author as subject for the reference collection, with a separate title/subject/first line catalogue to the extensive Broadside Ballad collection. There is a useful flip chart, *Index to the Quick Reference Collection,* a card catalogue for special collections, and an index of plays for women, while a wall chart and a computer print out provide guides to periodicals. The department has published its own guide to the collections and a typescript index to the Gaskell collection; the *Index of English Literary Manuscripts,* vol. 1, 1800 -1900, includes the holdings of the Central Reference Library.

Collections:
Reference material: An excellent range of encyclopedias, indexes, biographical and bibliographical works covering many topics and parts of the world. General works include *Index of English Literary Manu-*

scripts 1450-1900; Dictionary of Literary Biography; Prahbu Guptara, *Black British Literature, An Annotated Bibliography*; those specifically on women (a brief selection): Janet Todd, *A Dictionary of British and American Women Writers, 1660 -1800;* Wendy Frost and Michelle Valiquette, *Feminist Literary Criticism. A Bibliography of Journal Articles, 1975-81;* Dorothy Hilton Chapman, *Index to Poetry by Black American Women;* Diane Marting, *Women Writers of Spanish America. An Annotated Biographical-Bibliographical Guide.* Of particular interest among a wide range of periodicals is *Tulsa Studies on Women's Literature.* There is a good stock of second hand Victorian novels by women authors included among the reference collections. These were obtained by a librarian with particular interest in this field and can be found by following up authors in the catalogue.

Special collections: The Coleridge Collection covering printed correspondence, biographical, and autobiographical works includes many items by or about women literary figures. The Broadside Ballad Collection contains thousands of items from the 17th to the 19th centuries and is a noted source for studies of popular literature. The De Quincy collection includes Mrs Rachel Fanny Antonia Lee, *An Essay on Government* (1809), while an important miscellaneous volume is Anna Jameson, *The communion of labour. a second lecture on the social employment of women,* 1856. The autograph letter collection catalogued here, but available for consultation in archives, includes many items from women; for example, the authors Marie Corelli, Winifred Holtby, Storm Jameson; political figures Alice Jenkins of the Abortion Law Reform Association (1954, 56), Viscountess Rhondda (publisher of *Time and Tide*), 1948; Ethel Snowden, 1930s, Ellen Wilkinson, M.P., 1939-42. Other items concern women publishers such as Juliet Piggott, director of Curtis Brown Ltd, 1962. The department holds some manuscript items concerning Mrs Linnaeus Banks, and a major collection concerning Elizabeth Gaskell, incorporating the collection founded at Moss Side library in the 1890s. This includes some manuscripts such as letters, mainly about fundraising during the cotton famine (to be consulted in Archives), items from Mrs Gaskell's own library and several boxes of photographs and cuttings concerned with the celebrations for the centenary of her birth. Most of the collection consists of over 230 editions of her works, from rare first editions, to cheap reprints, and most of the critical studies and biographies in existence including copies of American theses.

Social Sciences Library: 061 234 1983/4

The library covers all branches of the social sciences and humanities except for literature, languages, art and music (see separate entries). It includes history, sociology, politics, social anthropology, social policy, law, education, geography, accounting, management and religious studies. Although financial cutbacks in recent years have hindered services and book purchasing, it has benefitted enormously from earlier decades of civic pride and generosity in one of the country's largest and best equipped public libraries. For those interested in women's history it is a rich and accessible resource. It has a notable collection of early printed books and particular strengths in 19th and 20th century printed books by and about women. It has many rare Victorian and early 20th century works relating to the early women's movement and has built up an equally good stock of 'new' women's studies material published over the past two decades. It functions as an undergraduate and research library as well as serving the general public.

Access: The library is situated on the first floor; the round reading room is served by a central counter where reference stock, whether books, periodicals, newspapers on microfilm material is issued. Service is quick and efficient, average waiting time being 10-15 minutes, except at busy periods.

Catalogue: Most reference material is in the card catalogues in the new catalogue hall on the first floor (see above). The catalogues are arranged by subject, author, and classification. A separate periodicals computer printout list is available in the reading room, at the central counter. Here you can also consult a list of all newspapers kept by the library.

Collections: are divided into three: open shelf lending stock for which a separate catalogue is available by the central counter in the reading room; reference stock on open shelves; reference stock kept in the stacks which must be ordered on request slips at the central counter.

Reference works: (on open shelves) Bibliographical material includes Short Title Catalogues from the 15th to the 19th centuries; Index of British Library Manuscripts; of the British Newspaper Library; Indexes of some national British newspapers and the New York Times; British Humanities Index; lists of theses. Official papers include for Britain, Hansard's accounts of parliamentary debates; official publications such as reports of Royal Commissions and Parliamentary committees, census returns on open shelves; similar material for some other countries is available from the stacks. Periodicals and reports from international bodies such as the International Labour Organisation are kept. Legal Publications include collections of statutes and Law Reports.

Biographical reference works such as *Who's Who, Dictionary of National Biography* (and similar works for other countries) are on open shelves. More specialised material such as *The Complete Peerage, Biographical Dictionary of English Catholics* is also kept. *Victoria County Histories, Keesing's Contemporary Archives* and other standard works of historical reference are also on open shelves.

Newspapers: The library takes most daily British papers, local news-papers and the *New York Times.* Current issues are in the reading room; back numbers, of daily and foreign papers are also available on microfilm in the reading room; back numbers of local newspapers are available from the Local Studies Unit.

Periodicals: There are extensive holdings of both historical and con-temporary material. There is a vast amount relevant to historians of women: the following is a brief selection illustrating the marvellous range of material. 'Domestic' women's magazines date back to the 18th century: a treasure trove can be found by looking in the index under

'Ladies', 'Mother', 'Englishwomen' - *Eliza Cook's Journal,* 1849-53, 1857-9; *Englishwoman's Review and Drawing Room Journal; Ladies Diary,* 1708-1839; *Lady's Realm,* 1896-1907; *Mother and Child,* 1931-1944. Periodicals concerning employment include *Domestic Servant's Advertiser,* 1913; *Industrial Newsletter for Women,* 1935-62; *Nursing Times,* 1933; T.U.C. Publications and Reports from 1882; *Woman Clerk,* 1919-21; *Working Gentlewoman's Journal,* 1909-10. Several titles concern education and teaching from late 19th century titles (*Journal* of the Women's Education Union; *Magazine* of Manchester High School for Girls) to the *Women and Education* of the 1970s.

19th and early 20th century socialist and political journals are well represented among the general political holdings. *Clarion,* 1891-1934; *Coop News* from 1871; *New Jerusalem* for 1827; *New Moral World* 1834-5, *Reformers Yearbook,* 1895 -1903; *Social Democrat,* 1897-1911; *Social Reformer* (Journal of the Manchester and Salford Independent Labour Party), 1899-1901. Various 19th century temperance and theosophy titles are held. There are publications from the major political parties including their women's publications (e.g. *Conservative Women,* 1921 -29). The Labour Party collection is especially comprehensive as is that of the Fabian Society with minute books (including those of the Fabian Women's group) as well as periodicals. The Communist Party women's paper of the 1970s *Link,* 1973-84 and *Socialist Woman,* 1969-78 are kept. Other important tiles: *Peace News,* 1967-; monthly newsheet of the Women's International League for Peace and Freedom, 1916-21; *Race,* 1968- and *Race Today* 1969-.

Feminist periodicals from both 'first' and 'second' wave feminism (and dates between!): *Birmingham Women's Liberation Newsletter,* 1973-5; *Birth Control News,* 1922-31; *Britannia* (official organ of the Women's Party), 1912-18; *Common Cause,* 1909-12; *Englishwoman,* 1909-21; *Englishwoman's Review of Social and Industrial Questions,* 1867-90; *Englishwoman's Yearbook and Directory,* 1899-1916; *Feminist Review,* 1979-; *Friends of Women's Suffrage,* 1914; *Manchester Women's Liberation Newsletter,* 1977-80; *New Voter,* 1929; *Red Rag,*

1972; *Sappho,* 1972; *Shrew,* 1971-83; *Spare Rib,* 1973-; *Suffragette,* 1912-18; *Suffragette News,* 1916; *Time and Tide,* 1920-78; *Woman Citizen,* 1923-45; *Women's Industrial News,* 1895-1919; *Women's Report,* 1972-3; *Women's Struggle,* 1970-1; *Woman's Suffrage Journal,* 1870-1890; *Women's Voice,* 1975; *Workers' Dreadnought,* 1914-24.

Jewish Library

This library, established in 1956, has now been closed and its stock dispersed through the Social Science Library and reference and lending sections of the Local Studies Unit. The stock consists of printed books, periodicals and annual reports of Jewish organisations. The catalogue of the original collection is by the central counter in the Social Sciences reading room.

Technical Library: 061 234 1987

On the first floor in the perimeter room or corridor around the Social Science reading room. It includes reference, open shelf and lending stock, books, periodicals, abstracts and indexes covering technology, medicine, science and engineering. There is a distinct card catalogue organised by author/title/subject/ classification and an information counter. The housewifery manuals of the late 17th century author Thomas Tryon are in the Technical Library. The **Patents Section** is also part of the library. An open shelf collection, it contains information on British, European and U.S. patents from the 19th and 20th centuries.

Commercial Library: 061 234 1991/2

On the ground floor; opening hours: Monday, Tuesday, Wednesday, Friday, 10 am - 6 pm; Saturday 10 am - 12, 1 pm - 5pm. Intended chiefly as a current information resource on business, finance and economic affairs generally with extensive on-line facilities for computer information searches. A European Information Unit is located within the Commercial Library. The Library is useful for recent information on women's employment and financial activities. It holds current issues of the *Financial Times*, foreign newspapers and a comprehensive range of commercial and financial periodicals including those dealing with industrial relations. There are trade directories, company information, statistical sources and telephone directories from all over the world. The Information Files, arranged alphabetically, include reports, press releases, statistics and so on, from the Equal Opportunities Commission, the European Community and the City Council on economic affairs. Headings such as 'trade unions', 'equal opportunities', etc are ways in to material relevant to women.

Chinese Library Service: 061 234 1970

This is primarily a general readers library for the Chinese community in Manchester. Books in Chinese are available for lending including adult fiction and non-fiction, together with Chinese music tapes, videos, compact discs and children's literature. Chinese newspapers, magazines and community information are available for reference. There is usually a Chinese speaking library assistant to help. There are books written in English about Chinese tradition and custom and bi-lingual materials are available. There is a small but significant number of books in English by or about Chinese women and on general issues of ethnicity and gender. Much more material by women authors on ethnicity and gender is available in Chinese.

Access: Located on the second floor; the library service shuts at 6pm on Tuesdays and Wednesdays and 5pm on Fridays. There is a children's play area.

Catalogue: Card catalogue arranged by author/title. Also a reference information index for selected subjects such as housing, travel, employment, race relations, equal opportunities and women (with information about Chinese women's groups in Manchester).

Collections: Reference works include Chinese and bilingual encyclopedias; pictorial reference works on China and Hong Kong such as *The Young Companion,* 1926 -45, and material on arts and crafts. Items of particular interest include, House of Commons Report , *The Chinese Community in Britain,* 1984-5; Jung Chang, *Wild Swans, Three Daughters of China,* 1991 (a non-fictional account of 3 generations of one family); Amy Tan, *The Kitchen God's Wife;* Tsai Chin, *Three daughters of China;* the autobiographical works of Han Suyin; Maria Liu Wong, *Chinese Liverpudlians, a History of the Chinese Community in Liverpool,* 1989; Haleh Afshar, eds, *Women, State and Ideology. Studies from Africa and Asia,* 1987; Sallie Westwood and Parminder Bhachu, eds, *Enterprising Women. Ethnicity, Economy and Gender Relations,* 1988;J.P.C. Pub, *Chinese Women Writers.*

Biographical material in Chinese includes, *Biography of Song Ching Ling* (Ren Min Pub); *Autobiography of Hong Xian Nu*; W.Q. Gui, *Biography of Jiang Qing;* Zheng Ji, *San Mo "Echos" World*; B.J. Luo, *Biography of Xiao Hong*; Qi Shu, *Ruan Ling Yu;* Ping, Ping Zhang, *Qui Jin.*

Local Studies Unit:
061 234 1979 (local history section)/1980 (archive section)

In 1991 the Local History Library and Archives were reorganised into the Local Studies Unit, located on the first floor of the library. Reorganisation has resulted in easier access and more convenient opening hours for archives users. Hours for the Unit are now the same as the general hours in the entire building although hours for consultation of archives are more limited; moreover it is **essential** to book a place in archives, and all the archives you wish to see at least 24 hours in advance.

Guides: (more detailed information on catalogues is given below). The unit provides a number of very useful leaflets and wall guides which help the reader to make use of the catalogues and to explore the library's rich local history and archival resources. Sample leaflets cover Family History Catalogue; Census Returns on Microfilm; Local Newspapers and Magazines on Microfilm.

Microfilm: Microfilm material is located beyond the new catalogue hall on the first floor. It is self service, with machines, film and indexes available to users on a first-come/first-served basis. First-time users should come to the main Local Studies Unit, for an explanation of how to use the self service area. Staff in the microfilm area can only give technical assistance, otherwise help should be sought from the Local Studies Unit itself (a telephone hotline is provided). Much local history material is available on microfilm and fiche: a brief selection includes local newpapers; census returns 1841-1891; rate books 1801-1901, for the central area of Manchester (a full set going up to the mid-20th century is available in Archives); Manchester telephone directories; directories (eg Slater's, Kelly's) for Manchester from the late 18th century to 1969, and some county directories for Lancashire and Cheshire, mainly 19th and early 20th century (additional county directories are available in the Social Sciences Library); quarter sessions order books, jury lists and other material from Lancashire County Record Office collections; miscellaneous manuscripts including theses.

Local History Section

For material, except original manuscripts, relating to the Manchester area. Some material including popular books and the volumes of local record and historical societies is available for lending. Most stock is reference only.

Catalogue: The card catalogue covers the Local Studies reference collection and also lists local material held elsewhere in the Library; it is organised by author, subject and classification number. Apart from this catalogue, which should be the starting point for research, there are two very useful card indexes:

Local information index is arranged alphabetically and leads to other sources of information. Subjects covered include places, buildings, institutions, companies, events etc., but not people or families who are listed in the separate Biographical index. The Information Index covers material in newspapers and magazine articles, and in the Miscellaneous Collection (MSC) of leaflets, newspaper clippings, brochures, information sheets, local election propaganda, and sundry items such as greeting cards.

Biographical index covers press cuttings and other material on local inhabitants. The index is arranged in one alphabetical sequence, by name of person or family. It provides access to material (eg obituaries) on prominent public women such as the suffrage leader and School Board member Lydia Becker (d. 1890); Manchester's first woman councillor Margaret Ashton (1856-1937) who was also active in the suffrage and peace movements, and in the Liberal and then the Labour party; the painter (Susan) Isabel Dacre (1844-1933); and the theatrical manager Annie Horniman (1860-1937).

Collections:

Printed material includes a comprehensive collection of books on all aspects of Manchester's history; parish registers and the publications of local record and history societies (eg Chetham Society; *Irish Heritage,* the magazine of Manchester's Irish education group, attached to the Irish Heritage Centre; *Manchester Region History Review)*; lending copies available.

There is a massive amount of more specialised local printed material especially useful for local organisations and the city council's activities; accessible mainly through the card catalogue under Manchester and its sub-headings (education, health, housing, politics, religious institutions, societies and so on). References are not consistent because they use titles current at the time of publication: Manchester City Council, Manchester Corporation, Manchester Education Committee would all be worth looking up for education, for example. There is a lot of useful cross referencing. Two drawers in the card index cover Manchester city and its corporation. Corporation committees include Education, Public Health, Maternity and Child Welfare, Social Services, Watch Committee. The material includes printed minutes, reports, pamphlets and press cuttings collected by the committees. They range from the publications of the Manchester committee for National Baby week, 1917, to those of the Police Monitoring Unit of 1980. Recent material covers the equal opportunities work of the Council, lesbian and gay initiatives and International Women's Week programmes.

There are printed minutes, annual reports, occasional publications of a whole host of voluntary organisations: examples include Annual Reports of the Manchester Women's Christian Temperance Association, the Governesses Institution and Home (1864 -1901), the Manchester Gentlewoman's Work and Help Society; Manchester Women's Institute Report and Accounts (1877); the Business Young Ladies Association of Manchester (1884-1930). Annual Reports of Manchester, Salford and District Women's Trade Union Council, 1895-1919; and Annual Reports of the Manchester and Salford Central Association of Societies for Girls and Women (from 1896 known as the Union of Women Workers, Manchester, Salford and District Branch), 1891 -1895, are important sources for organised women of the late 19th, early 20th centuries. Poor Law and Workhouse Records, mainly from the late 19th century include Year Books of the Guardians of the Manchester and Prestwich Union; Chorlton Union Manual, all mainly late 19th century. The printed records can often be supplemented by archival material.

There are many annual reports, and press cuttings etc from local hospitals and other medical institutions and this is the best starting point for research into the history of organised health care for women (see also separate section on Manchester medical records). The printed records of educational institutions, charities, churches (which often had ladies' committees - Mrs Gaskell was active in the affairs of Lower Mosley Street chapel and its schools); official celebrations (eg royal visits, coronations), societies, and theatres all provide useful sources for the history of women. The headings 'lesbian' and 'gay' offered mostly news-cutting material, with some items of council activity. The general headings in the subject index are often better than the specific ones concerning women ('work', for instance, has some useful sub-headings on women's work, whereas women's work as a main heading elicited few references). As always ingenuity is needed. There is some material, mostly recent, on Black and Asian women in Manchester: a cutting about Abasindi, a black women's organisation based in Moss Side; the productions of the Black Writers' Workshop and the newsletter of the Sikh Union of Manchester are examples.

Extensive **print collection** indexed by subject, name, and topographically (ie specific parts of Manchester). This also includes material on other parts of Greater Manchester, Lancashire, Cheshire and Derbyshire.

Broadsides and posters indexed by subject and date - includes material from the 16th century onwards produced in, or concerning Manchester.

Large **map collection** - with index organised by area and date.

Archives Section

Access: These are rich collections but very understaffed. They are open to everyone but space is currently limited to 10 readers each day, and you need to book a place in advance. All material has to be ordered at least 24 hours in advance. Archives are available Monday - Wednesday, and Friday, 10am - 7.30pm; catalogues and lists can be consulted whenever the Unit as a whole is open. (N.b. some literary manuscript material is available in the Language and Literature Library).

Catalogue: Unless you are coming to see a specific, major collection the card **indexes** are probably the best places to start - they are organised by name, place and subject. Further details on the collections are in the red/orange files holding calendars and lists of each collection; these give further detail of the collections mentioned below. Items with the prefix C deal with Cheshire, L with Lancashire, M (the bulk of the material) with Manchester, O with other counties. The subject index is one of the best we've seen - very detailed, with much cross referencing; but as always imagination is necessary - there is a wealth of relevant material not to be found under the heading 'women'. The cards concerning 'women', along with sub-headings including education, employment, political parties, rights, societies, do yield useful references. Other good ways 'in' are to look up places (Manchester includes the sub-headings politics, poor relief,societies, Sunday schools, theatres...) and topics like diaries, domestic service, wages, industry, poor relief, prophecy, prostitution, trade unions.

Collections: We have highlighted promising examples from the wide-ranging collections.

Public bodies: Local government records of Manchester from the medieval manor to the city corporation are available here.
M91/: ancient records of the manorial court leet.
M116/: Manchester Quarter Sessions Records 1839 -1951- for minor criminal offences (has references to prostitution, for example); prior to 1839 Manchester had no independent Quarter Sessions court but was part of Salford Hundred of Lancashire: records for Manchester (covering poor relief, minor crime etc, are at Lancashire Record Office,in Preston).
M117/: petty sessions records, from 1839, include material on brothel keeping.
L27/: material on prisoners in Salford's New Bailey prison 19th century.

Poor Law material: M3/: Manchester 'old' Poor Law records: M3/3/1, overseers' account books from 1663; M3/9/1-613, apprenticeship indentures 1700-1813: there is a very full calendar of these records giving apprentices' names, masters and trades.
M4/1-94, records of the Guardians of the Poor for Manchester, Chorlton

and Prestwich Unions, 1842 -1930; then records of Manchester Public Assistance Committee (later Social Welfare Committee) 1930-48; M4/2, are weekly statistical returns of Manchester Union including details of numbers of inmates, and covering Blackley, Manchester and Prestwich workhouses; M4/52/1-28, are Chorlton Union weekly returns 1844-1910.

M10/: further Poor Law material, among the records of townships now part of Manchester, including overseers' accounts, under the old Poor Law: M10/7/2/1, for example, is Cheetham overseers' accounts, 1693 -1791.

L89/9/1-16: Stretford Poor Law material: overseers' accounts, settlement certificates and examinations, mid-18th century.

Education: M65/: School Board records 1870 -1903 (nb women could sit on School Boards and as Poor Law Guardians before they could be members of the general City Council). The suffragist Lydia Becker was a member of Manchester School Board 1870 -1890.

M66/: records of individual Manchester local authority schools.

[N.b. further material on women and education can be found in the records of churches, and other voluntary organisations especially for the period before 1870: M41/, for example, is the records of the Ladies Jubilee Female Charity School.]

The city council's own proceedings are printed in full; committee proceedings can be traced in brief through 'Epitomes' or summaries available in the main Local History section. If more detail is required, minutes of committees etc can be ordered by name and date of committee through the Archives section.

Family papers: Those with particularly promising material on women include:

M35/: Papers of the Worsley family of Platt Hall from the 16th to the 19th century include: marriage and other settlements; wills, household accounts, letters (e.g. of Elizabeth Norman 1780s-1830s on health, family and public affairs); sermon notes from the 1630s.

M173/: Papers of the Fyldes family of Newton Heath, a family of grocers and corn merchants active in religious, charitable, and educational bodies. Interesting material concerning women members of the family includes the diaries of Emma Fyldes Buckley of Bradford 1909-15; correspondence relating to the appointment of staff in local schools; involvement of family members in local Conservative politics.

M473/: Papers of the Lomas and Murgatroyd families of Manchester and Heaton Norris, prominent Methodist families, include much material on 19th century women members (eg the writings and correspondence of Elizabeth Lomas, b. 1826).

Diaries in the subject index include:

C21/2/1,2: Clara Alcock, Sunday School teacher b. 1855; diaries covering 1874-5, 1877-80.

MISC/339, 1819 diary of an anonymous Manchester woman.

MISC/505: diary of Helen Boardman, cook, 1906 -32.

MSF 920.7 W80: diary of Anna Walker, soldier's wife, 1789 -1814

Public figures:

M14/: the papers of Lady Simon of Wythenshawe concerning education and local government, from the 1920s to the 1960s.

M220/: the papers of Hannah Mitchell, 1906 - 1955, Independent Labour Party activist, suffragette, local councillor and JP.

Misc/718: papers of Annot Robinson, 1892 -1925, peace worker and suffragette.

Suffrage: The best known collection for women's history in the library is M50/. There are two bodies of material:

1: the papers of the Manchester branch of the National Union of Women's Suffrage Societies [NUWSS] and the North of England Society for Women's Suffrage [NESWS] with additional material relating to the International Women's Suffrage Alliance, parliamentary division lists and bills.

2: the papers of Millicent Garrett Fawcett (President, NUWSS)

This is an extensive collection of papers relating to the suffrage movement, particularly the NUWSS, and to a wide range of women's organisations of the 19th and early 20th centuries such as the International Council of Women, the Education Reform League, the Society for Promoting the Return of Women as Poor Law Guardians, the Moral Reform Union, the Manchester and Salford Women's Citizen Association, the Women's Trade Union Provident League, the Society for Promoting the Employment of Women. The collection has material covering campaigns for the education of women, their employment, health and welfare as well as suffrage. Looking up prostitution in the subject index yielded interesting references from this collection.

M131/: Manchester Branch of the National League for Opposing Women's Suffrage, papers.

Women's organisations:

M82/: Soroptomists Papers.

M162/Box 54 [see also M136/2/3/3600] Papers of the Manchester Ladies Anti-Slavery Society.

M271/: National Council of Women records, including material from the Women's Citizen Association and many other groups: M271/5, National Council of Women discussions on the child and the cinema 1927-8 (found under 'children' in subject index); M271/8 is the papers of the Married Women's Association, Sale.

M290/: Records of the Women's Gas Federation.

M350/: Women's Zionists Societies.

Women and welfare:

M15/: Ardwick Nursery

M126/: Manchester and Salford Sanitary Association records from 1852; its Ladies branch has minutes, visitors' reports etc.

M184/: Records of the Manchester and Salford Council of Social Service (a coordinating body for voluntary organisations). This collection includes the records of the Mothers' Guild and School for Mothers, 1908 -1935; Homes for Women, 1938-1970; Citizens' Advice Bureaux 1939 -45 as well as of more recent voluntary bodies.

M427/: Home Helps Society

MF 2687: Minutes of the Jewish Sanitary Association (Jewish Ladies Visiting Association) 1884-1898.

Political organisations:
M42/: Minutes of the Manchester Branch of the Independent Labour Party, 1902 -19. Women played an active part in the Manchester ILP which was also the seed bed for the suffragette Women's Social and Political Union [WSPU]. M42/2 is the records of the Clarion Club, 1913 - 21.

M137/8/1,2: Pamphlets and leaflets for local government and parliamentary elections, 1892 -1920.

M128/2: Material relating to the Withington Conservative club, male only before 1918, mixed thereafter. Pre-1918 minute books contain references to women's activities in an auxiliary capacity, for example, in the Primrose League.

M283/8/1/1,2 Records of the Manchester Liberal Women's Central Council 1924-1938. M283/9 covers local Manchester Groups.

M301/5/2/2: Manchester City Council Labour Group: a chronological and biographical record, 1894 - 1966.

M313/: Papers of the Joint Disarmament Council. (Includes at M313 / 3/8 women delegates from the Women's Cooperative Guild to a peace conference; and material from the Women's International League for Peace and Freedom).

M435/: Ardwick Labour Party records, 1970s.

M449/: Manchester Labour Women's Advisory Council Minutes, 1928-1943.

M450/: Gorton Labour Party Women's Section Minutes, 1929-34, 1941-45; Openshaw Women's Section Minutes 1947-58

M455/: Wythenshawe Communist Party, 1970s.

MSF 310.62 M1, minutes, MSF 310.6 M5, reports of the Manchester Statistical Society, in which several women social reformers were active.

Women and work:

M488/: Manchester Branch of the College of Midwives Material 1929 -83 (restrictions on material less than 30 years old).

M493/: Manchester Teachers Association Records 1874 -1964; M494 has the records of the Manchester District Union of Elementary Teachers 1871-1904.

MF 2836-37: Microfilm of Pamphlets and Leaflets of the Waterproof Garment Workers Union, 1934-62. Women worked in this trade, particularly in Jewish areas of Manchester.

L1/: The Farrer antiquarian collection, is a broad collection of Lancashire material; it includes material on wages in the cotton industry and on poverty in the 19th century, for example the fascinating notebooks of Ann Ecroyd, on the relief of the poor by Marsden Society of Friends Poor Relief Committee, 1819 -1853 (L1/2/24/1-67)

Manchester City Art Galleries
Mosley St and Princess St,
Manchester M2 3JL
Tel: 061 236 5244
Fine Arts Senior Keeper : Sandra Martin
Decorative Arts Keepers: Ruth Shrigley (metalwork and furniture)
and Lesley Jackson (ceramics, glass, and 20th century design)

Type of institution: Collection of public galleries, including the main site at Mosley/Princess St, plus Wythenshawe Hall, Heaton Hall, Queen's Park Conservation Studios and the Gallery of English Costume at Platt Hall (see separate entry for Platt Hall). The City Art Galleries are divided into two sections: Fine Arts includes sculpture, prints, drawings and paintings; Decorative Arts includes ceramics, glass, metalwork, textiles, furniture, wallpapers and oriental objects.

Access: The Mosley/Princess St Gallery is open Monday - Saturday 10am - 5:45pm, Sunday 2 - 5:45pm; mostly inaccessible to wheelchairs. Galleries at Heaton and Wythenshawe Halls (disabled access to ground floors) are open only in summer. Telephone main number for details. Researchers must make an appointment with the keepers, preferably at least 2-3 weeks in advance, since material is stored at outlying galleries.

Collections: Many of the items in both the Fine Arts and the Decorative Arts collections have been donated by women patrons. The **Fine Arts** collection is catalogued in the following publications, which can be found in the Arts Library in Manchester's Central Reference Library, and in other public libraries:

Concise Catalogue of British Paintings
I Artists born before 1850 (1976): A portrait by Angelica Kauffman (1793), a landscape by Sarah Dodson (1901), self-portrait by Louise Jopling, and numerous paintings by Isabel Dacre (1844-1933) and

Annie Swynnerton (1844-1933), founders of the Manchester Society of Women Painters.

II Artists born after 1850 (1978): Some 80 women artists are represented, most by one painting. Those with more than one work in the collection include Marion Adnams, Vanessa Bell, Ethel Gabain, Edna Genesi, Gwen John, Therese Lessore, Flora Reid and Ethel Walker. Also notable is the World War II work of Evelyn Dunbar and Elsie Hewland.

Concise Catalogue of Foreign Paintings (1980): Five European and one Brazilian artist represented.

Catalogue of the Permanent Collection of Paintings (1903): Same as concise, but contains biographical information on artists like 'the popular battle painter' Elizabeth Butler, Angelica Kauffman and Fiona MacDonald Reid.

Concise Catalogue of British Watercolours and Drawings I (1984): More than 75 women's watercolours and drawings; Marion Adnams, Helen Allingham, Kate Greenaway, Edna Clarke Hall (designs for 'Wuthering Heights'), Margaret Kaye, Therese Lessore, Emily Gertrude Thompson, and Lily Florence Waring are all represented by more than two works each.

There is no published catalogue of the prints collection, but nearly 50 women artists are represented, with lithographs, linocuts, engravings, woodcuts, etchings and aquatints. The following are represented by more than two works: Joan Ellis, Stella Langdale, Clare Leighton, Therese Lessore, May Aimee Smith, Ethel Spowers, Caroline Watson, plus engravings after Angelica Kauffman.

Sculpture holdings are small, but include works by Barbara Hepworth, Elizabeth Andrews, Christine Kowal Post and others.

All told, the collection holds works by more than ninety women artists, only four of which are on permanent display. For further information about the collection, enquire in writing.

Portraits of famous women in various mediums include Isabel Dacre's of suffrage campaigner Lydia Becker, and others of 18th century and 19th century actresses like Lady Hamilton, and public figures like Caroline Norton. Portraits of local women include artists Isabel Dacre and Annie Barnett (an 'amateur artist', by Adolphe Valette), and professional women Caroline Herford, lecturer at Manchester University and a magistrate, and Margaret Ashton, first woman councillor of Manchester.

Representations of women by male artists abound, including some relatively realistic portrayals -- like the 17th century 'Sir Thomas Aston at the death-bed of his wife', and the factory workers in 'The Dinner Hour at Wigan Mill'. But most images are romanticized, notably the very young and nubile women in the gallery's large collection of Pre-Raphaelite paintings. See further Griselda Pollock's alternative guide, 'A Feminist Looks Round the City Art Gallery'.

The **Decorative Arts** collection has no printed catalogue, but gallery publications *A Century of Collecting* (1983) and *Porcelain from Europe* (1986) cover a range of collections. Card catalogues and lists for all collections are available at Mosley/Princess St; enquire in writing.

Held at main site: extensive ceramics collection, with many 20th century pieces by women, including Clarice Cliff, Susie Cooper, Stella Crofts, Marion Dorn, Janice Tchalenko and Katharine Pleydell-Bouverie; glass collection (very contemporary) including works by Annette Meech, Ann Warff and other women; Assheton Bennett silver collection, including pieces by six 18th century and three 20th century women; enamel collection of 300-400 mid-18th century to mid-19th century boxes, nut-graters, snuffboxes, etc.

Work by many 20th century women makers and designers is represented in a new permanent collection display called 'A New Look at Decorative Art', as well as in the temporary decorative art exhibitions in the Ground Floor Galleries.

Held at Wythenshawe Hall: furniture collection; wallpaper collection, including some designed by women in the 1950s; Mrs Greg's 'Bygones' collection (1922) of small tools like thimbles, wool winders and pastry cutters, plus hornbooks, pattens, pincushions, dolls and dollhouses, and more. (Most of the papers of the Tatton family of Wythenshawe Hall are held at the John Rylands Library at Deansgate and the GMC Record Office.)

Held at Heaton Hall: furniture collection; material relating to the actress Fanny Kemble. (The papers of the Egerton family of Heaton Hall are held at the GMC Record Office.)

Gallery of English Costume
Platt Hall, Platt Fields
Manchester M14 5LL
Tel: 061 224 5217
Keeper: Anthea Jarvis / Assistant Keeper: Miles Lambert

Type of institution: One of the Manchester City Art Galleries. Only a small number of the holdings are on display at any one time. *The Fabric of Society 1770-1870,* by former keepers Jane Tozer and Sarah Levitt, (published by Laura Ashley, 1983) provides an introduction to the collection.

Access: Gallery open Monday to Saturday 10am-5.45pm (except closed Tuesday), and Sunday 2-5.45pm; closes 4 pm November to February, inclusive. Library open Monday to Friday 10am -5pm, by appointment only. Disabled access to ground floor only (library upstairs).

Catalogue: Card catalogues of the costume collection are classified under women, men, and children (and by item of clothing within each of those categories), accessories (fans, gloves, etc), and other textiles (samplers, etc). Drawings and engravings also have a card catalogue. The paintings - none by, but many of, women - are listed in Appendix I of the published *Concise Catalogue of British Paintings,* covering all the City Galleries.

Collection: The costume collection includes a few items from the late 17th century, but most date from the mid-18th century to the present day. The vast majority of pieces are women's clothing (the interest of C.W. Cunnington, whose private collection founded the museum in 1947), and they represent predominantly middle and upper-class dress until the mid-20th century. However there are a number of items of nurses' dress, some servants' clothing, and a few pieces of suffragette paraphernalia.

In addition to items of costume, there are books, periodicals, paper patterns and shop books, photographs, private papers, and paintings, etchings and engravings. The book collection includes secondary sources on costume, textiles, needlework, dressmaking and tailoring, plus etiquette books dating from the early 19th century to the present day. The periodicals collection is impressive, including women's journals from the mid-18th century to the present day, some of which are downmarket, plus tailors' journals from the 19th century. Particularly 'good runs' include *L'art et la mode* (1955-65), *La belle assemblee* (1806-63), *Englishwoman's Domestic Magazine (*1853-79), *Eve* (1919-29), *Gentlewoman* (1890-1920), *Girls' Own Paper* (1880-1903), *Graphic* (1870-1902), *Home Chat* (1890s-1910), *Home Fashions* (1917-44), *Housewife* (1940-46 and 1959-68), *Illustrated London News* (1842-1916), *Lady's Magazine* (1774-1829), *Lady's Monthly Museum* (1798-1809), *Lady's Pocket Magazine* (1824-39), *Lady's Treasury* (1857-91), *The Lady* (1885-1965), *Lady's Realm* (1897-1908), *London Magazine* (1734-81), *Punch* (1841-1930), *Queen* (1862-1963), *Tailor & Cutter* (1868-1929), *Vogue* (1915-92), *Woman's Weekly* (1945-54 and 1956-61) and *Young Ladies' Journal* (1867-96). There are many other journals with a smaller number of issues. The keepers would like to hear from anyone interested in cataloguing the women's magazine articles by subject.

The paper pattern collection covers the entire life of the commercial dress pattern from the 19th century to the present. The 20th century shop books illustrate ready-made clothes.

The photographs begin in the 1840s and their subjects are primarily middle class, but there are some nurses and Welsh women iron workers. The miscellaneous papers are few: wills, inventories, etc of the 18th century and 19th century illuminating certain aspect of dress. Paintings, etchings and engravings illustrate costume from the 18th century to the 20th century.

Art Galleries

There are other city art galleries within the area covered by this survey which we did not visit in person. All of them hold oils, watercolours, drawings and prints by women artists.. The smaller galleries - Bury, Oldham, Stockport - have works by up to 25 women. Almost all of these artists date from the mid-19th century to the present and most are represented in any collection by only one work. While few paintings are on display at any time, the keeper will answer enquiries and have lists of works by women artists.

Bury Art Gallery, Textile Hall, Manchester Road, Bury.
Oldham Art Gallery, Union Street, Oldham.
Stockport Art Gallery, Greek Street, Stockport SK3 8AB.

Information on these galleries was kindly shared with us by Adrienne Wallman, of Blackburn City Art Gallery, who has organised a travelling exhibition of women's pictures in 1993, using works from North West collections, including those at Blackburn, Blackpool, Bolton, Burnley, Lancaster, Preston and Rochdale, as well as those in Greater Manchester. For the women in the art galleries in Liverpool, see the catalogue of the 1988 *Women's Works*, by Jane Sellars (National Museums and Galleries on Merseyside).

East End anarchists, including three Witcop sisters, c. 1920, courtesy of the Manchester Jewish Museum

Manchester Jewish Museum
190 Cheetham Hill Road
Manchester M8 8LW
Tel: 061 834 9879
Curator: Catharine Rew

Type of Institution: This private trust run museum is housed in a former Spanish and Portuguese synagogue built in 1874 in the heart of what was once Manchester's main Jewish district. It tells the story of the Jewish community in Manchester over the last 200 years with an emphasis on social history. The collections consist of photographs, oral history tapes, secular and religious objects, pamphlets, textiles, manuscripts and a few printed books.

Access: Hours are Monday to Friday 9 am - 4.30 pm; Sunday 10.30 am - 4.30 pm. Researchers are welcome, but an appointment must be made in advance as there is limited space. Disabled access but not to all parts of the museum.

Catalogue: The main collection of artifacts and archive material (books, pamphlets and original photographs) is indexed on computer according to the following categories: simple name (e.g. certificate, photograph, memorial board, textile, ceramic), detailed name (e.g. ladies' coat, nationalization certificate, identity papers), provenance (name of institution), date of item and subject (e.g. industry). The catalogue is a closed system in that only the archivist may use the computer. Most material is catalogued according to the SHIC system (Social History Information Catalogue) which uses four main headings - domestic and family life, working life, community life, and personal affairs - with further subdivisions.

Collections:
Photographic collection: c. 17,000 items mainly dating from the 1880s to the present day. Many have been copied from family albums

and therefore reflect the museum's general interest in life history. The collection is catalogued by card index according to donor and name. Varied documentation consists of deposit sheets providing information about the donor, biographical information about the subject and cross references to other materials in the museum such as printed papers and tapes. Photographs are stored in the form of small contact prints; most have a Manchester connection, but some depict ancestors and homelife in central and eastern Europe.

Oral history tapes: Over 300 tapes - more than half with women interviewees. There are transcripts for nearly a third, and the subject index has a separate women's section. North West Sound Archives (Clitheroe) has copies on cassette which may be used by researchers at GMC Record Office; it has compiled a key word index and a computer-ised index of names, date of birth and place of origin. These are life history tapes of people from different social groups; interviewees are either first or second generation, and most have some connection with Manchester. All aspects of life are covered - education, childbirth, marriage, childhood, home and family life, work, leisure, Zionism, political and trade union activity, religion, charitable and voluntary work. A new oral history project on the holocaust is currently underway.

Textiles and artifacts: These consist of religious items for use in the home and in synagogues relating to rituals and festivals such as Passover and the Sabbath - e.g. matzo covers, tapestries, tablecloths, crockery, candlesticks. Workplace items include equipment used in the tailoring and garment trades which employed many Jewish girls and women.

Archive material: Because of limited storage space, much of this material is housed at the GMC Record Office, but must be consulted at the museum. Holdings are varied and include personal papers such as identity cards, Red Cross wartime letters, passports, ration books, naturalisation certificates, journals and letters. There is also Jewish material, mainly on institutions, at Manchester City Archives.

Manuscript material of interest includes: a copy of a register of deliveries in Cheetham belonging to midwife Dora Black (1913-14); the Harris House Diary - a journal containing short essays, 'Our First Year in Harris House, 1939-40', written by residents of Harris House, a wartime hostel in Southport for mid-European Jewish girls who came to Britain on their own; letters (d. 1923-25) from the pupils of Sarah Marks, teacher at the Jews' School in Cheetham until her marriage in 1925; scrapbooks of B'nai B'rith, a Jewish charity which had a women's section.

A travelling exhibition called **Women of Worth - Jewish Women in Britain** was produced in 1992 in conjunction with the London Museum of Jewish Life. It contains a high proportion of Manchester material and can be hired for display. A booklet is also available from the museum shop.

Tailoring workshop of Philip Weitz, East End of London, c. early 20th century, courtesy of Manchester Jewish Museum.

MANCHESTER MEDICAL RECORDS

As hospital records are scattered in various libraries and archives offices as well as still found in the hospitals themselves we have included a brief general account of them.

For further information see L. Coyne, D. Doyle and J. V. Pickstone, *A Guide to the Records of Health Services in the Manchester Region* 2 parts, occasional publications no. 3-4, Department of History of Science and Technology, UMIST (1981).

The Central Reference Library holds much material for the principal Manchester hospitals including comprehensive material for Withington Hospital, and Annual Reports and press cuttings for St Mary's and Manchester Royal Infirmary. This would be the starting point for most research on medical institutions. The records of the Eye Hospital are in Greater Manchester County Record Office. The **Manchester Medical Collection,** part of the Main Library of Manchester University has rich holdings of medical books and extensive Annual Reports for hospitals and nursing institutions in the city. There is much material on maternity and child welfare services as well as information on women as health workers and dispensers of charity. Deansgate also has important medical material (see entry). However, the records of the Duchess of York Hospital for Babies went to Withington Hospital when the Babies hospital was closed. This hospital was founded by women doctors to promote their medical opportunities as well as to improve babies' health and its history is of major importance.

Manchester Royal Infirmary
Oxford Road
Manchester, M13 9WL,
061 276 1234

Type of Institution: NHS teaching hospital, founded as voluntary hospital in 1752.

Access: The archives department of the hospital is irregularly staffed; contact the librarian about hours and times. Disabled access possible with help, please contact the librarian in advance.

Catalogues: Coyne, Doyle and Pickstone (see above) offer the best listing of records.

Collections: There is a wealth of material on the day-to-day running of the hospital; records go back to its founding. Administrative records include annual reports (1752-1966), weekly and general board minutes (1752-1949), Ladies committee minutes (1935-45) and many others. Employment aspects of nursing are well-documented in Nursing Committee minutes (1929-1938), nursing salaries and wages data (1871-1947, not complete) and the nurses register (1878-1956). Information about hospital patients is contained in admissions registers (1752-1878, not complete), gynaecological admissions registers (1878-1908, not complete) and a range of other specialized admissions registers, including details of the eighteenth-century lunatic patients. Case notes are scarcer: one set each, surgical (1886-95), and medical (1875-78).

St. Mary's Hospital
Whitworth Park,
Manchester M13 OJH
061 276 1234

Type of Institution: NHS teaching hospital for women and children, founded as a maternity charity in 1790.

Access: The Archives are not staffed and may shortly be moved to the Central Reference Library. Access should be sought through the Hospital Secretary.

Catalogues: The archives were listed in Coyne, Doyle and Pickstone (see above).

Collections: Administrative records include annual reports (1790-1947, not complete); quarterly and weekly board meeting minutes (1790- 1905, not complete), midwifery training committee minutes (1940-65) and many more. Midwives' own records include a case book (1886-92) records of deliveries (1945-69) and Miss Lovatt's Flying Squad calls (1948-51). There is a large collection of patient records, such as a variety of in-patient and district maternity registers from the first half of this century, and a collection of case books covering most of the period 1878-1913, and one from 1938. Miscellaneous records such as scrapbooks (1938-49), photographs from the interwar period, registers of midwife pupils 1853-1910 (note: these are housed in the John Rylands University Library of Manchester Medical Archive), and nursing/midwifery training registers from 1923, afford an unusually rich portrait of an institution and of urban maternal health and welfare.

Manchester Metropolitan University Library
All Saints Building
Oxford Road, Manchester M15 6BH

Humanities, Art and Design Librarian: Gaye Smith 061 247 6108
Social Sciences Librarians: Miraenny Boughen and
Jane Simister 061 247 6106

Type of Institution: University library (formerly Manchester Poly-technic) mainly serving the needs of undergraduates but with some interesting special collections of 19th century periodicals, fashion magazines, greeting cards and common place books. The archive also holds the records of the former Art College.

Access: Open to own members and staff and students from other Universities on production of identity documents. Access by non members at the discretion of the University Librarian. No access for school students. Opening hours are: Term, Monday to Thursday 9am - 9pm; Fridays 9am - 5pm; Fridays (November to May) 9 am - 7 pm. Special collections/archives 9am - 4.45pm (by prior appointment). The library is also open on Sundays from 10am - 4pm from November to May (term time only) for reference purposes - ring in advance to check. Disabled access with assistance. Photocopying facilities.

Catalogue: The main catalogue is computerised and provides access to books and periodical holdings. Some special collections have separate indexes.

Books and periodicals: The library's periodical collection has strengths in 19th century material, particularly general women's magazines, and in fashion magazines - haute couture rather than everyday fashions. There are good secondary sources relating to the textile industry and women artists. There are two excellent guides to the periodicals collection: Tricia Meech, *The Development of Women's Magazines 1799-1945* (1986); *Fashion Textiles and Women's Periodicals* (1985).

76

The library subscribes to *Studies on Women Abstracts*, a useful abstracting service for women's studies, mostly in the social sciences.

Special collections/archives: Material relating to the history of women in art education, Manchester women artists, and printed records of the former Art College, such as annual reports. The collection is strong for the Victorian period, but more patchy post-World War I. For student records, enquire at Administration in the All Saints Building. Also of interest are the *Seddon Collection* of Victorian and early 20th century greetings cards and the *Page Collection* of Victorian scrap albums and common place books.

Hollings Library
Manchester Metropolitan University
Old Hall Lane, Manchester M14 6HR
Librarian: Wayne Connolly
Tel 061 247 6118

Type of Institution: One of the Manchester Metropolitan University Libraries serving the Hollings Faculty which includes the Departments of Clothing Design and Technology, Food and Consumer Technology, Hotel Catering and Tourism Management.

Access: As main site. Opening hours are: Term: Monday to Tuesday 9am - 8pm; Fridays 9am - 5pm; Fridays (November to May) 9am - 7pm. Vacation: Monday -Friday, 9am - 4.30pm. Visiting researchers by appointment.

Catalogue: The main catalogue is computerised (as main site).

Collections: There are c. 27,000 volumes: Main subjects - Clothing Technology, Food Technology, Hotel Management, Hotel and Catering. Related subjects: Law, Industrial Relations, Management. Main area relevant to women relates to women and fashion design at 746.92.

Abstracts, indexes and bibliographies (Selection relevant to women): British National Bibliography, British Humanities Index, Clothing Index, Fashion Index, Anbar Abstracts.

Periodicals (Selection relevant to women): *Apparel Industry Magazine, Body Fashions/Intimate Apparel, Draper's Record, L'officiel de la couture et de la mode de Paris* (1978-), *Vogue* (1975-), *Womenswear* (continued by *International Colour Authority: Womenswear/Menswear*), *Women's Wear Manufacturer* (formerly *Maker Up*, continued by *Manufacturing Clothier*).

Clothing theses: Selection of student theses on subjects related to clothing and consumer issues.

Archives collection: Contains a good deal of material on Elsie Hollings (the college principal for many years) who received the OBE for her activities for the war effort, e.g. she founded the Aid to Russia Fund in World War II.

Other Manchester Metropolitan University site libraries: Didsbury Library serves the School of Education and contains children's literature and the Morton Dandy collection of school textbooks.
Elizabeth Gaskell site Library holds a collection of historic cookery books and an archive on domestic science education in Manchester.

The Manchester Museum
University of Manchester
Oxford Road
Manchester M13 9PL
Tel: 061 275 2634
Director: Alan Warhurst. Keeper of Egyptology: Rosalie David

Type of Institution: Museum, run by Manchester University in cooperation with local authorities. Its collections were begun by Manchester
Natural History Society and Manchester Geological and Mining Society
and transferred to Owens College (the precursor of the University) in
1868.

Access: Open to the public Monday - Saturday 10am - 5pm. All groups
should book in advance. Intending researchers should write in advance
to the Director or the relevant Keeper. For disabled access there is a lift
and helpful portering staff.

Catalogues: The books and periodicals from the Museum's own library
are included in the main University library catalogue although most of
the material is kept in the Museum. For the many lists of collections and
the Museum's archives it is best to consult the specialist keepers. The
correspondence of successive Keepers of Egyptology, for example, is
listed by date and name. The Museum's catalogues are currently being
computerized.

Collections: The main collections of the Museum amount to over 9
million objects and are the richest in the north of England. They cover
Archaeology; Egyptology; Ethnology, Entomology, Botany, Geology,
Numismatics and Zoology. There is also a rich collection of archery
material. The Ethnology and Archaeology sections contain a variety of

resources for investigations into the lives of women in different cultures. Religious artifacts, textiles and domestic items from America, Africa, Asia, Australia, and the Pacific Islands are available for consultation.

The Egyptology material was collected through systematic excavation rather than purchase and provides a particularly rich source, especially if used in conjunction with the papyri in the Deansgate Library and the textiles collections of the Whitworth Art Gallery. Egyptian women were comparatively well educated and had a relatively high legal status; they worked as professional mourners, in textiles and in bread -making. In addition the Museum's own archives and its collections of books and periodicals have great potential for the history of women in Manchester. There are sources for investigating the role of women in higher education and museum work, again especially in Egyptology where five women have served as Keepers of Egyptology: Margaret Murray (on secondment from University College, London) 1908-12; Winifred Crompton (1912 -1932); Mary Shaw in the later 1930s; Elise Baumgartle in the 1940s and Rosalie David at present. Murray and Crompton in particular were pioneering women in a pioneering period for their discipline; the museum's archives include their correspondence with the prominent Egyptologist Flinders Petrie, his wife Hilda, and their daughter Ann. In general the letters of the women keepers are useful for the working lives of academic women.

The Journals of local learned societies kept by the Museum, many no longer in existence, such as the Manchester Egyptian and Oriental Society (of which Crompton was secretary) provide some information of the involvement of local women in the intellectual and associational life of the region in the nineteenth and early twentieth centuries.

Manchester Studies, Oral History Tapes
Manchester Metropolitan University
Cavendish Building (North)
Cavendish Street
Manchester M15 6BG
tel: 061 247-1765
Contact: Dermot Healy

Type of Institution: This is an archive of oral history tapes collected by the former Manchester Studies Unit. The tapes are of interviews made with people who lived and worked in the North West, and cover a wide range of topics; childhood, marriage, school, work, leisure, politics, trade union activity, etc.

Access: The tapes and related documentation are currently held in Tameside Local Studies Library. The tapes are in storage and must be ordered in advance, but the transcripts and summaries can be consulted at any time during library opening hours (see entry for Tameside Library). Appointments to hear tapes and general enquiries should be made through Dermot Healy at the above address.

Catalogue: There are summaries for all the tapes and full transcripts for about half, which are arranged alphabetically by name. There is an index which identifies the nature and purpose of the interview, but there is no subject index as such.

Collections: The following tapes may be of interest:
Women in the cotton industry - interwar and pre-war.
Political activity in the inter-war period - mainly left-wing.
Maternity and health campaigns in the inter-war period.
Women's family experiences, poverty, housing and domestic service.

The Museum of Science and Industry in Manchester
Library and Record Centre
Liverpool Road, Castlefield
Manchester M3 4JP
Tel: 061 832 2244
Senior Archivist: Ann Jones
or Archivist: Elizabeth Sprenger

Type of Institution: The Library and Record Centre is the searchroom and study area for the Museum. The Centre houses archives, photographs, drawings and printed materials. The main focus of the collections is Greater Manchester and the region, especially energy industries, engineering, textiles, avaiation, science, photography, and scientific instruments. It also holds two collections of national scope, on electricity and on paper-making. For women's history, the collection is of interest for its material on women workers, and a wealth of material relating to the production, marketing, and consumption of domestic technologies.

Access: Researchers welcome Tuesday and Thursday, 1 pm - 4.30 pm, and by appointment at other times. Disabled access is good. Admission is free to those who make an appointment.

Catalogue: The Centre has a card index to books, journals and trade literature. Individual collections are catalogued in a series of handlists, some have finding aids. Not all collections are fully catalogued yet; the archivists are very helpful and researchers would do well to consult them first. See also the brief article in the *Manchester Regional History Review,* IV, Spring 1990.

Archival material: The two national collections are those of the electricity industry and the National Paper Museum paper and water mark samples. The first contains much material on the domestic use of electricity, including the Electricity Council Archive (1957-1990); the printed materials of the Electrical Association for Women (ca. 1880s-1970s) a consumer group; the Electrical Development Association (1919-1960s), an industry pressure group concerned with standards and coordination. The minutes of the EAW are held by the Institute of Electrical Engineers (Savoy Place, London WC2R OBL; 071 240 1871) but the printed materials include magazines, etc. An overview of the activities of the EAW and the EDA is contained in the paper, 'Persuading the Housewife to Use Electricity?', by Pauline Webb and Elizabeth Sprenger, *Journal of the British Society for the History of Science,* forthcoming. The Jenny Webb collection contains the papers of a demonstrator for electrical appliances who became the head of domestic appliance testing for the Electricity Council. They include teaching manuals from the 1950s. There is information on women's wages in the electrical industry 1915-1950 contained in the industry's records of industrial relations bodies. There are records of women's wartime employment in the Beyer-Peacock locomotive makers records, including photographic material. The records of Glover, of Trafford Park, include photographs and other records of women employed to operate braiding machines used in cable making. The Centre also contains the archives of the Museums's own development.

Printed material: As well as printed material contained in the collections above, the library also holds trade catalogues, manuals, company histories, and histories of friendly societies and trade unions. There is a collection of domestic magazines, such as *My Home* and *Ideal Home* from the 1920s-1950s. There are various ephemera relating to domestic management, such as wartime cookbooks, catalogues of domestic appliances, etc. There is a trade literature collection built up by a painter and decorator. Many of the journals may hold references to women, for example a collection of aviation magazines may touch on women and flying.

A library of contemporary and older books covers the spectrum of the Museum's interests. It includes books relating to women and technology.

National Museum of Labour History
103 Princess Street
Manchester M1 6DD
Tel: 061-228 7212
Keeper of Collections: Myna Trustram (museum collection)
Librarian: Stephen Bird
Archivist /Researcher: Andrew Flinn (archives)

Type of Institution: This is an independent museum with collections covering the organised labour movement of the 19th and 20th centuries and which eventually will portray a social history of the working class.

Access: Monday - Friday, 10am - 5pm. All researchers are welcome by appointment. The Archive Centre is keen to provide access to local GCSE students engaged on project work. On Mondays when the museum is closed, entry should be made by the side door in Hart Street. Disabled access is possible with assistance. From Spring 1994 the museum's main public galleries will be located at the Pump House, Bridge Street, Manchester. The Archive Centre, however, will remain at 103 Princess Street.

For administrative purposes the collections are divided into two: those of the Archive Centre and those of the museum.

Archive Centre

Catalogue: The majority of the collections are catalogued by standard archival handlists with name and subject indexes. There is a continuing process of computerisation whereby the old lists and newer collections are being entered onto a database for ease of searching.

Collections: The archive contains the **Labour Party Archive** and the museum's own archival collections. There are specific collections relating to women in the Labour Party as follows: Women's Labour

84

League; Standing Joint Committee of Industrial Women's Organisations; Annual Reports of the National Conference of Labour Women; *Labour Woman*; the papers of individuals such as Marion Phillips and Mary Middleton (the latter containing items about domestic service, child welfare, and maternity) material relating to women's trade unions. Other material can be found in the general correspondence and General Secretary's files. Women's section material can be found in the subject files which also contain items pertaining to international women's organisations, the Women's International League for Peace and Freedom, women on juries, women's work (1916-23), women's rights and suffrage (1916-25). For the post-war period the General Secretary's file has material on Mary MacArthur Holiday Homes, Barbara Castle and Sylvia Pankhurst.

Other items of interest include the Raya Dunayevskaya (founder of 'Marxist Humanism')-Harry McShane correspondence (1959-1988); Ellen Wilkinson's scrapbooks; material on the Women's International Congress Against War and Fascism; records of the women's section of the Chilean Solidarity Campaign. There is also a collection of pamphlets. The archive of the Communist Party (Great Britain) will be available from Spring 1994.

The following items are available on microfilm: *The Freewoman*, 1911-1919; *Suffragette* 1912-1918; *Woman Worker*, 1908-1910; *Woman's Dreadnought*, 1914-1924; 5 reels of microfilm of Sylvia Pankhurst's writings, and her work with the W.S.P.U. in East London. The minutes of the National Executive Committee and the Annual Reports of the Labour Party are on microfilm which is available in libraries around the country. The records of the Independent Labour Party are also on microfilm.

Although the archive has some local material, this is being distributed to local record offices for which a list will be available eventually. The Archive Centre's own guide is being updated.

Museum

Catalogue: The bulk of the museum collection is on a computerised catalogue system. A highly selective but useful guide to the collection can be found in John Gorman's *Images of Labour* (Scorpion 1985) and *Banner Bright* (Scorpion 1986) available at the museum.

Collection: This consists of photographs, artifacts, memorabilia, works of art, ephemera and banners.

Photographic collection: Photographs are accessible in the form of contact prints. There is a subject index, with an entry for women, subdivided as follows: strikes, unionism; demonstrations and meetings, sweated industries, the Anti-Sweating League, Cradley Heath chain makers, agricultural workers, coal workers, the garment trade, women workers in the first world war, housemaids, prostitution, women's shelters, American female labour, millworkers, women campaigning for equal pay and protesting against unemployment, suffragettes, the Women's Social and Political Union, the East London Federation of Suffragettes, various political and trade union figures such as Marion Phillips, Julia Varley, Mary MacArthur, Labour Party women's sections. It is also worthwhile cross-referencing with other categories - for example, political movements - for references to the Clarion movement and socialist parties such as the Social Democratic Federation (there is one photograph of a woman selling the SDF paper, *Justice)*. Some mounted photographs portraying domestic labour, sweated industry and women's suffrage can be borrowed. The museum also has a collection of portraits.

Artifacts: The collection includes Women's Co-operative Guild material such as trophies, leaflets, posters, membership cards, commemorative mugs; Socialist Sunday School material; Independent Labour Party material, such as badges, rosettes, posters, leaflets; a widows' weeds outfit donated by the Dockers' Union; a replica of the National Federation of Women Workers banner; Greenham Common material; 1984/5 Miners Strike Women's Support Groups ephemera.

Daily News Sweated Industries Exhibiton, 1906, courtesy of the National Museum of
Labour History

North West Film Archive
Minshull Building
Manchester Polytechnic
Minshull Street
Manchester
Tel: 061–247 3097/8
Curator: Maryann Gomes

Type of Institution: This is a regional public moving image archive containing films, videotapes and television programmes about the North West from 1896 to the present day. The Archive is part of the Manchester Metropolitan University and is funded by North West Arts Board, AGMA, Lancashire and Cheshire County Councils, Granada Television and BBC North.

Access: Open to the public and interested researchers by appointment. Hours are 9am - 5pm Monday to Friday. Viewings and access are either free or subject to a scale of charges, depending on residence, and/or intended use of material. Copyright and donor restrictions operate in some cases. The Archive provides particular services for schools, societies, museums, galleries and reminiscence groups in the region and since 1990 has produced a range of videocassette merchandise. Disabled access by arrangment.

Catalogue: The Film and Video Catalogue is maintained on a computer database and holds details of over 1,000 titles. Material can be found by title, date, producer, place or subject (or any combination) and detailed written descriptions are available for over 50% of them. A less detailed index is available for collections awaiting inspection - also computerised. Researchers will be assisted. A printed catalogue of c400 titles is available in local history libraries in the North West and a second edition is in preparation. Publications of interest are: *The Picture House: A Photographic Album of North West Film and Cinema* by Maryann Gomes and the *Researchers Guide to British Newsreel Collections* published by the British Universities Film and Video Council.

Collection: The Archive's acquisition policy pertaining to the North West is to collect documentaries, newsreels, publicity/promotional films, television programmes, home movies/videos and corporate productions. The collection is particularly strong in urban, industrial coverage up to 1950. Themes particularly illustrated include work, transport, sport and leisure, entertainment, celebrations, shopping, healthcare, housing, streetlife, childhood experience, and wartime life in the region. Whilst many titles feature women's lives, few films are known to be made by women. Of particular interest are films made for the Co-operative Wholesale Society during the inter-war years with titles such as 'Her Dress Allowance' (1930) made for promotional purposes.

Researchers could also approach Granada Television and BBC North which are located in Manchester and have their own film libraries.

North West Sound Archive Listening Station
c/o Greater Manchester County Record Office
56 Marshall Street
New Cross, Manchester M4 5FU
Tel: 061 832 5284

Type of Institution: The North West Sound Archive is a local government based organisation, associated with Lancashire Record Office, and based at Clitheroe Castle, in north Lancashire. It would normally be outside the geographic scope of this guide; however, as copies of the archive's extensive tape collection can be listened to at the GMC Record Office we have included the following information. The Sound Archive collects material recording 'the history, traditions, language and culture of the north west of England' and is the most extensive in the United Kingdom outside London, with over 80,000 recordings in its collections.

Access: Recordings are available on loan by post or can be listened to at the GMC Record Office during normal opening hours and by arrangement. Copies of some tapes are stored here; others must be ordered from Clitheroe (GMCRO staff will do this for you). Contacts at Clitheroe are Ken Howarth, Andrew Schofield, Lynda Yates, tel: 0200 27897; North West Sound Archive, Clitheroe Castle, Clitheroe, Lancashire, BB7 1AZ; fax: 0200 26339, marked for the attention of ''Sound Archive''.

Catalogue: The main catalogue is stored on computer at Clitheroe; users can contact the archive for an initial subject search, which is free. A print-out of available material is sent, for a selection to be made. Alternatively, initial searches can be made at GMCRO where there are copies of the catalogue, printed and on cassette which is very useful for blind researchers. The indexes are arranged by subject, name and keyword - the latter giving the date of the interview but not the subject matter. Researchers are advised to consult both indexes as neither is fully comprehensive. For example, the subject index lists material under suffrage, but the keyword index does not. However, the subject catalogue does yield a great many references under 'women' and is therefore a good starting point. There is also a separate catalogue called, 'Voices in the Crowd', for a BBC Radio Manchester programme of the same name in which ordinary people were interviewed. The tapes are listed by occupation, eg 'below stairs woman', 'fish wife', 'flapper', 'head-mistress', 'hospital matron', 'suffragette', 'Tiller Girl'.

Collections: The Collections cover many aspects of Women's History, including the textile industry, pit-brow lassies, Marie Stopes, female M.P.s, suffragettes, education, professions, nursing, childbirth, homelife. The following are interesting examples selected from the subject index in Manchester. Cotton manufacture - interviews with women from local mills. Coal mining - interview with Nellie Potter who worked at the pit-top at Maypole Colliery, Wigan, in the early 20th century. Mary Kershaw of Rochdale - writer of dialect prose and songs. Violet Carson - broadcaster, actress and musician. Labour Party - interviews with women M.P.s, Ann Taylor and Judith Hart. Suffrage - interviews with suffragettes and members of the Pankhurst Trust. Gracie Fields - recordings of her songs, and interviews. General Strike, 1926, - textile industry, unemployment and state help. Education - life in a boarding school near Southport in 1918. Fairfield Moravian Settlement at Droylsden. Third World Women's Conference - girlhood in Grenada; the Nicaraguan revolution. Bangladeshi Women and Children's Asso-ciation. Long Moss Asian Women's Cooperative - interview with Manchester Councillor Nilofar Siddiqui. Hiroshima - Marie Bowland, member of WILPF (Women's International League for Peace and Freedom) recounts her experiences.

Life history tapes refer to the more obvious broad areas of schooldays, family life, leisure and work, but also contain specific references such as memories of Little Ireland in Manchester, the Queen Victorian Jubilee Celebrations and life in a common lodging house. Some of these tapes will be found under the subject heading 'women', but other interesting material was found under such diverse headings as: 'Fairs, Carnivals, Whitwakes and May'; 'Sewers, sanitation, public health'; 'Diseases'.

Oldham Local Studies Library
84 Union Street
Oldham
Tel: 061 678 4654
Local Studies Officer: Terry Berry
Archives Officer: Paul Sillitoe

Type of Institution: Public library and borough archive serving the Pennine community of Oldham and district which is well-known for its 19th century cotton mills. In addition to a good stock of local history and local government material, the library has an extensive photographic collection. The archive contains the records of local societies, organisations and firms, material about the social reformer Mary Higgs, and the important Lees Collection which includes items relating to suffrage, local government and women's organisations.

Access: Hours are Monday, Wednesday, Thursday, 10am - 7pm; Tuesday 10am - 1pm; Friday 10am - 5pm; Saturday 10am - 4pm. All researchers welcome, including school students. The Local Studies Officer has a particular interest in women's history and women's suffrage. Disabled access is possible via a ramp from Greaves Street. Photocopying available. Those needing a microfilm reader should book in advance.

Catalogue: There is a well referenced card index system arranged by name, subject, useful information, photographs, newspaper cuttings, wills, obituaries, and archive calendars. The library produces its own introductory leaflets and has a wide range of local histories and guides for sale.

Collections:
Local history material: There are parish registers, census returns, maps (e.g. parish tithe and estate maps) and newspapers - including the *Oldham Chronicle* (Liberal, 1854 to date), the *Oldham Standard* (Conservative, 1859-1947), the *Oldham Express* (1867-1886), the

Oldham Times (1860-1863) and other short-lived and specialist titles. Transactions of local societies relevant to Oldham and district include those of the Chetham Society and the Saddleworth Historical Society. The open shelf stock contains a good range of local history material such as printed books, street and trade directories, Reports of the Inspector of Factories for Lancashire (1835-40) and an unpublished account by Frank Pogson of his childhood in Oldham from 1924-39, 'A Ginnel to Life', with detail about his mother, schooldays, leisure and work. Collections worth investigating are the Butterworth Manuscripts which includes a diary of daily events in Oldham (1829-1843), the Rowbottom Diaries, recording daily events from 1787-1829, and the Elsie Beech Collection (Misc 44) - research notes (1930s) and unpublished books by a local historian who wrote about the Radcliffe family of Chadderton.

Photographs: There are over 20,000 photographs with some excellent suffrage pictures, others depicting women in local mills, at the spinning wheel, gleaning coal during the 1924 General Strike, etc. A copying service is available.

Local Government Records: The library has council minutes for Oldham Metropolitan Borough, and other records for the districts of Oldham, Chadderton, Crompton, Failsworth, Lees, Royton, Saddleworth, Springhead and Uppermill, and the parishes of Woodhouses and Bardsley.

Church and Chapel Records: These include a number of Church of England and Nonconformist registers (on microfilm) for local congregations: Wesleyan, Methodist, Congregational, Baptist, Unitarian and Moravian. Also of interest are the records and minutes (1919-83) of the Excelsior Gospel Temperance Mission; records of the Lord Street Unitarian Chapel (1888-1947) and the Royton Congregational Church (1894-1983); and records of the George St Independent Methodist Chapel (1811-1906), including a register of members, account book and sunday school minutes. Some church records date back to the 16th century.

Business, Employment and Trade Union Records: See the Coldhurst Mill Collection (Misc 41) (1875-1962) including wages books, index of personnel and benefit records; the Werneth Ring Mills Ltd Collection (Misc 42) (founded 1874) has staff records; the Holyrood Mill Co Ltd Collection (Misc 47) includes wages books for 1949-55. The Oldham Trades and Labour Council (Misc 17) has deposited minutes and annual reports. The family records of Hilda Pearson (Misc 29) who worked in the cotton industry were deposited by the former Manchester Studies Unit.

Society Records: There are records for a number of co-operative societies in the Oldham area. Also of interest are the annual reports and minutes (1936-79) of the Oldham Moral Welfare Council, with the records of the Oldham and District Marriage Guidance Council (Misc 4) (1946-52).

Personal and Family Papers: The Crompton papers (17th - 19th century) have a few items of interest such as deeds, wills, a rent book belonging to Mary Schofield for 1866-74, and family letters. There are deeds of local women - mainly spinsters and widows - from the 18th and 19th centuries. See also the Holland Collection (Misc 24) which has papers relating to Mary Carter (1923-25).

Political Papers: See the Ethel Rothwell Collection (Misc 50) - Mayor of Oldham and Conservative councillor in the 1950s and '60s; and material relating to Annie Dickson (Misc 11), an Oldham suffrage activist who took part in the Suffrage Pilgrimage of 1913.

Mary Higgs, (Misc 13) (1854-1937) was a social reformer who campaigned for women's lodging houses and lived amongst the homeless in order to experience their conditions of life. She moved to Oldham with her husband, a Congregational minister, founded the Beautiful

Oldham Society (an urban regeneration scheme) and was a member of the Oldham Council of Social Welfare. The library has biographical newscuttings about her life and work, a few annual reports of hostels founded by her, and copies of her writings, including poems, pamphlets and books.

Lees Collection: Dame Sarah and Marjory Lees of Werneth Hall, Oldham were active in a broad range of political, public and voluntary campaigns and organisations, particularly in the first decades of the 20th century. Sarah Lees, a local councillor, was elected mayor of Oldham in 1910; Marjory was active in the suffrage movement. The collection contains diaries, letters, notes, newscuttings, photos, etc, referring to local authority matters, the Women's Local Government Society, public health, women's suffrage, Liberal politics, women magistrates, Poor Law Guardians, the Women's Citizens Association, Manchester University Settlement, the National Union of Women Workers (later, the National Council of Women), the Women's Co-operative Guild, birth control clinics, prostitution, temperance, pit brow lassies, nursing, Women in Council, The Central Committee for Women's Employment (1914), the League of Nations Union, the National Peace Council. Correspondents include Mary Stocks, Margaret Llewelyn Davies, Mary Higgs and soldiers at the front in World War I. There are annual reports and other records of the Oldham Women's Citizen Association and other organisations, as well as issues of *The Women's Leader and the Common Cause* (1929-31). Also of interest is an unpublished thesis by Terry Jane Berry, 'The Female Suffrage Movement in South Lancashire, with particular reference to Oldham 1890-1914', MA Huddersfield Polytechnic, 1986.

Two photographs showing women from Oldham on the Suffrage Pilgrimage, 1913,
courtesy of Oldham Local Studies Library

Portico Library
57 Mosley Street, Manchester M2 3HY
Tel: 061-236 6785
Librarian: Jo Francis

Type of institution: A private subscription library and newsroom founded in 1806 for the 'new' middle classes of Manchester. Its predominantly 19th century and early 20th century stock contains collections of travel literature, fiction, biographies, and a small number of social and political essays by women authors. Also of interest are the Library's archives and its 19th century printed catalogues. There is an exhibition gallery open to the general public.

Access: Open Monday to Friday, 10 am to 4:30 pm by appointment, and restricted to those engaged in professional research either in higher education or independently. Both the Library and small reading room have great charm and character and provide a peaceful alternative to the busy Central Reference Library in nearby St Peter's Square. No disabled access. Photocopying.

Catalogue: The card catalogue has separate indexes arranged by subject, author/title, voyages and travels, biography, 19th century and North West fiction. The catalogue employs a unique system dating from the early 19th century, consisting of two letters and a number, and will eventually be computerised. The subject index has a few items under headings such as 'witchcraft' or 'women', but as usual, creative use must be made of the entire catalogue. There is as yet no comprehensive guide to the Library's stock of works on or by women, although an excellent printed list of books by 19th century lady travellers has been compiled, and the librarian would like to hear from researchers who might wish to catalogue other specialist parts of the collection.

Of particular interest are the Library's 19th century printed catalogues for the original collection of books and pamphlets, of which only a small proportion remain. The catalogues are of great value in their own right as bibliographical aids in the search for material by and about women. Their detailed subject guides are arranged by headings such as Arts &

Sciences, Domestic Economy, Voyages and Travels, Politics, Pamphlets, and Polite Literature (e.g. dictionaries, rhetoric and romances). A trawl through the indexes can bring to light many lost treasures and forgotten authors.

Collections:

Portico Archives. These are papers relating to the history and administration of the Library, and provide insight into the class and gender nexus of 19th century cultural institutions. Women were excluded from full membership until 1892; they could enter the Library and participate in social functions, but had no borrowing rights. From the 1890s women became more prominent in the Library's affairs, with the first woman librarian being appointed in 1945. For a full history of the Library and its place in Manchester's cultural life, see Ann Brooks and Bryan Haworth, *Boomtown Manchester 1800-1850. The Portico Connection* (Manchester, 1993). It includes a chapter on women.

19th Century Lady Travellers: This collection of c.165 books must be one of the best in the country. It contains works written by, or about, 19th century lady travellers, from the well-known to the obscure, including the 1856 edition of Isabella Bird, *The Englishwoman in Africa*, the 1863 edition of Mrs Atkinson, *Recollections of Tartar Steppes and their Inhabitants* and the 1892 edition of Kate Marsden's account of nursing in Russia, *On Sledge and Horseback to Outcast Siberian Lepers.*

Printed Books. The Library's general collection includes social and political works by Frances Power Cobbe, John Stuart Mill, Josephine Butler, Eliza Lynn Linton and an excellent collection of works by Harriet Martineau. The fiction list includes Fanny Burney, Rhoda Broughton, Margaret Oliphant, Maria Edgeworth, Mrs Henry Wood, Frances Hodgson Burnett and many lesser known authors. Other items of interest include: *Industrial and Social Position of Women in the Middle and Lower Ranks* (1857); *A Contemporary Narration of the Proceedings of Dame Alice Kyteler, Prosecuted for Sorcery in 1324*, ed. by Thomas Wright (1843); *Home Life of English Ladies in the XVII Century* (1860); *A Guide to the Unprotected in Everyday Matters Relating to Property and Income,* by a Banker's daughter (1863).

Type of institution: Independent museum since 1976 in the cotton mill run by the Greg family from the late 18th century (buildings now owned by National Trust). In its time the mill was considered a model of industrial responsibility for its treatment of workers. The property includes the mill buildings, the apprentice house where child workers lived, and the factory village of Styal. The apprentice house is open for 'living history' every Monday, when schoolchildren dress up and learn to be apprentices (contact the education officer for details). The booklet *Mill Life at Styal* by Nigel Nixon and Josselin Hill, is available in the shop and provides an introduction.

Access: To archives, Mon-Fri 10am - 5pm , by prior appointment; to museum, April-Sept 11am -5pm, Oct-March 11am - 4pm but closed Mondays. Wheelchair access is limited to lower two floors of mill and lower floor of apprentice house; no charge for mill. Phone ahead for further information on disabled access.

Catalogue: Documents, photocopies, and related articles and prints are catalogued by subject, under entries like 'cotton manufacture and trading', 'education', 'health and welfare' (including accident and death lists), 'enquiries into conditions', 'trade unions', 'legislation', etc.

Collection: Both the social welfare and the business records of the mill survive, and since the Gregs preferred female employees because they were cheaper and more reliable, there is much material here. Or rather there would be if the original records hadn't been broken up, some going to Chester Record Office and some to Manchester Central Library. Quarry Bank has a list of the material in Manchester, but not in Chester. Quarry Bank's own collection includes some original documents, some photocopies of documents at Chester and Manchester, secondary material, and photographs. The Greg Collection comprises the business records: accounts, cash and wage books, registers of workers, doctors' visits, age and school certificates, apprenticeship indentures, and correspondence. Unexpected original documents include the travel diaries and sketch books of the Greg daughters' trip to Eqypt in the 1870s, and the diary of a nurse in the First World War. The Shawcross Collection, named after the superintendents of the apprentice house, consists of the social welfare records: details of the apprentices' food, schooling, health, etc. in the period 1794-1847. The secondary collection includes books and journals on technical aspects of textile production, a good collection of museum periodicals, and the contents of the now-defunct Styal village lending library. The photographs are boxed by subject: people in Styal village, workers, other mills, textile machinery (both factory and domestic), water power and water courses, the Greg family, and museum developments.

Rochdale Arts and Heritage Department
Local Studies Section,
Central Library, The Esplanade, Rochdale,
Tel. 0706 864915
Assistant Librarian, Local Studies: P.Godman

Type of Institution: Public Library founded in 1874 and situated on its present site from 1884. The Local Studies Collection comprises a wide range of books, maps, pamphlets, photographs, documents and audio-visual material relating to Littleborough, Milnrow, Castleton, Wardle and Norden, as well as to the Rochdale area. Following local government reorganisation in 1974, the historic boroughs of Middleton and Heywood were annexed by Rochdale. However, both retain their own libraries with important local history collections.

Access: Hours: Monday, Thursday, 9.30am -7.30pm; Tuesday, Friday, 9.30am -5.30pm; Wednesday 9.30am -5pm; Saturday 9.30am -4.00pm. Parking available at Town Hall nearby. All welcome. Photocopying and microprinting facilities. Disabled access with help from companion or library caretaker.

Catalogue: The very informative booklet, *The Local Collections: An Introduction,* covering Middleton and Heywood as well as Rochdale is now out of print but can be consulted in the Library. Archives are listed by topic (Educational Records; Family and Private Papers, Local Administration, Political Records etc). Many of the archives are at present in rather inaccessible storage and should be ordered well in advance. A computerised list of books, pamphlets, newspapers, handbills, photographs etc is being prepared. Much of this material is on open shelves, organised topically (local histories, biographies etc) so browsing can be very productive. Staff are extremely knowledgeable and helpful.

Collections: The library holds copies or originals of census returns, parish registers, non-conformist registers, electoral rolls, souvenir programmes and brochures, local almanacs and directories, wills, and other material vital for local history. There are over 600 local maps.

A comprehensive collection of local newspapers includes *Rochdale Recorder* (1827-8), *Rochdale Observer* (1856 to date); *Rochdale Times* (1827-1924) and several monthly and weekly titles from the 1840s. Press cuttings and miscellaneous material for many topics have been arranged in box files ('Gracie Fields'; 'Health'; 'Housing'; 'Ethnic Minorities' and so on). The file on ethnic minorities begins in 1941 but is fuller for the 1970s onwards with good coverage of Rochdale's Asian community, recent Vietnamese settlers and the poor conditions suffered by young Filipino women brought to work in a local mill in 1971-2. A compilation, 'A Woman's Place' is made up of current material and extracts from the archive collection.

Other printed source material includes the reports and minutes of local voluntary and public bodies such as Friendly Societies and the Charity Organisation Society; Chief Constables Reports from the 1880s; Transactions of the Literary and Scientific Society, which had several women members; medical, church and educational material. Amongst many hundreds of books on the Rochdale area are collections of autobiographies and work by local authors, such as John Collier (the dialect writer, 'Tim Bobbin'); and many good local histories such as those by William Robertson, writing in the late 19th, early 20th century; and, more recently, John Cole. A useful collection of general secondary works covers politics, trade unions, housing etc, Virago reprints and works on women's history with a local dimension such as Patricia Hollis, *Ladies Elect*. The library holds copies of many theses written on Rochdale, notably Michelle Abendstern, 'Expression and Control: A Study of Working Class Leisure and Gender, 1918 -1939' (Essex University Ph.D, 1986); and the productions of local history societies such as the Heywood Living History Group.

Photographs: some 7,000 items including many fascinating representations of women working in textiles, munitions and the forestry corps in world war one; in Rochdale Infirmary in 1897; as chainmakers, smiths, laundry students, barge-women. Local 'characters' include wise women and Mary Alice Hartley (d. 1879), also known as 'Ailse O' Fussers', last of the 'lime-gal drivers' who owned a string of packhorses carrying lime and coal across the moors. There is an extensive collection of broadsheets, theatre posters and political handbills, including suffrage and election material.

Numerous **films and videotapes** record local events from 1913; oral history resources include tapes produced by the North West Sound Archive and local groups, as well as material collected by the library. Amongst other items these record the memories of a local suffragette and an Asian woman's early experiences in Rochdale.

Archive material includes: material from the Cooperative Society, founded in Rochdale, - some also at the Coop's Toad Lane museum in Rochdale. Company records include records of textile mills (such as the Era Mill Company, 1897-) where many women were employed, often acquired when companies went into receivership in the 1980s. Educational material includes school log books and school board records and also trade union records, such as the Minute Book of the Rochdale Women Teachers' Association, 1917 -1934. Family papers include correspondence by and to women (eg from the Chadwick, Leach and Tweedale families in the Robert Leach papers). Poor law material illustrates the activities of women guardians while the usual records of municipal committees survive, including minutes of the Maternity and Child welfare sub-committee for 1929-31, but some have been contaminated by asbestos and are unavailable. Some legal records are kept with various restrictions on access for reasons of confidentiality. Health records include reports of Medical Officers of Health (some on open shelves) and hospital records. Amongst material for Rochdale Infirmary going back to the 1890s, are records of the Ladies Committee while further evidence of women's philanthropic activity is found in the records of the Poor Children's Aid Committee from the 1870s. There is material on relief work and suffering during the Cotton Famine of the

1860s. Trade Union records - of the Cotton Spinners Union, the Rochdale Weavers' Association and other textile and metal working unions are well known but have not been fully utilized by historians of women. Political material is especially plentiful for the Labour Party and the Liberal Party: there are records of Women's Liberal Associations for Rochdale (1896-1906, 1917 -1927) and Castleton (1920-1939). Other promising material includes letters from young evacuees in the Channel Islands during the second world war; and records from the town's rich theatrical and music hall traditions.

Croft Mill Museum
Hamer Lane
Rochdale
Tel: 0706 41085.
Museum Services Officer: Debbie Walker

The holdings of the museum overlap with those of the local studies collection and include photographs, posters, advertisements, nineteenth century remedy booklets (often written by women), diaries, correspondence, especially from the first world war, valentines and postcards from the late nineteenth century, postcard portraits of textile workers in both work and holiday clothes, besides costumes, textiles from many cultures, and domestic implements. Women have been involved in the creation of these collections and others covering geology, and Egyptology. There is no general guide or catalogue as yet but one is being produced for schools loans exhibitions. Staff are extremely anxious to make the material available and travelling exhibitions are organised.

Gracie Fields Archive and Temporary Exhibition:
A key archive of visual material and objects relevant to the life and career of Gracie Fields is held by the Rochdale Museum. A temporary exhibition presenting this material in the context of the film industry and the lives of working class women in the North West is on show in Rochdale.

Rochdale Art Gallery

Rochdale Art Gallery has researched and curated exhibitions of women's art from the 18th century to contemporary work of an international focus. The gallery maintains an archive of slides, video, research material of women's work, accessible to the public and to scholars. Research includes representations of women in 19th and 20th century art and photography and addresses issues of class, gender, sexual politics and race.

The 'Laundry Class' in Rochdale Technical School, 1901, courtesy of Rochdale Libraries Service

John Rylands University Library of Manchester
(On two sites, on Deansgate in Manchester city centre, and on the
Main Campus, Oxford Road).
Librarian: Mr C.J. Hunt.

Type of Institution: The John Rylands University Library of Manchester was formed in 1972 through the merger of the university library with the private John Rylands Library, Deansgate. The combined Deansgate and 'Owens' (or main campus) holdings form the third largest university library in Great Britain and one of the major scholarly libraries of Britain, or indeed the world. The Deansgate Library houses most of the 'special collections' but some archive material is housed at the main site on Oxford Road, which also has extensive microfilm holdings as well as newspapers, periodicals and printed book collections.

Guides to Material:
Detailed and separate entries for Owens and Deansgate are provided below, but some guides cover material in both. The Library produces a Student's Guide and a series of subject guides - on History, English and the like. There is a more substantial 'General Research Guide' and an on-going series of valuable guides to resources in specific areas (Guides are available for English, French and German Studies, Theology and Church History, British History). The summer issue of the *Bulletin of the John Rylands University Library of Manchester* is devoted to the Library's collections. A regularly updated leaflet, 'Recent and Forthcoming Publications', gives information about new exhibition catalogues, research guides and so on, and is available free from the Library.

The Main Library
John Rylands University Library of Manchester,
Oxford Road,
Manchester M13 9PL
Tel: 061 275 3738

Type of Institution: University Library for undergraduate, postgraduate and academic readers.

Access: Readers need a University Library Card. In general, lending rights and inter-Library loan facilities are confined to past and current members of the University. Non-members of the University wishing to use the general Library must apply in writing or in person to the Librarian. Archives users, especially if travelling from outside Manchester are advised to enquire by letter or phone, as some material is kept in store and is therefore not immediately accessible. Visitors should make initial enquiries at the Ground Floor Information Desk. Full disabled access to all parts of the building. Photocopying facilities are mainly on the ground floor. Opening hours:
term and Easter vacation: Monday - Friday 9.00am - 9.30pm; Saturday 9.00am - 1.00pm.
Christmas and summer vacations: Monday -Friday 9.00am - 5.30pm; Saturday 9.00am -1.00pm.
Archives and microfilm material can only be ordered during counter service (until 5.00pm weekdays), but microfilm can be reserved and used during all opening hours. Many information services are not available in the evenings or on Saturdays.

Catalogue: The catalogue hall on the ground floor has a card catalogue arranged by author/title. There is a separate card catalogue for medical material (including the history of medicine). A computer version of the main catalogue is accessible from terminals throughout the Library. The computer facilities have recently been updated to make subject and thematic searches easier. The computer can indicate whether a book is on loan or not but does not necessarily include all older material. Books

105

received since summer 1992 are recorded only on the computer catalogue. In addition there are card indexes to the Library's archives
holdings (including those kept at Deansgate), newspaper holdings and
(by accession number) to microform material. There is a computer print
out of periodical holdings and a guide to the periodical holdings of other
Manchester libraries.

There is no central archives office, and researchers are best advised to
start with the General Research Guide, Collections Location Guide,
individual handlists of collections and specially prepared leaflets (eg
Reader Guide GS. 1, Labour Party Library Collections), all of which are
available at the Ground Floor Information Desk. Staff at the Information
Desk are not always familiar with the Library's archival holdings, but
if you need more detailed information or assistance with your search you
should ask to see a member of the archives staff. The archivist is Dr
Dorothy Clayton, tel. 275 3757.

Collections: In our description of the Libary's holdings, we have
focused on the most specialised material, but there is also a vast amount
of general secondary and reference material vital for students of
women's history, as for many other topics.
The women's studies/women's history stock of printed books is reason-
ably good and expanding, subject to financial constraints; they cover a
range of themes such as family, work and politics, and geographical
regions, such as the Americas, Africa and Asia as well as Britain and
Europe. Periodicals taken include *Feminist Review, Feminist Studies,
Women's Studies International Forum,* and *Signs;* but financial problems have limited the acquisition of recent titles. Much bibliographical
material is available on the ground floor, often in microform including
British and American Books in Print, while the reference section on the
first floor includes a comprehensive selection of abstracts, biographical
and bibliographical guides and citation indexes.
The British Humanities Index, British National Bibliography, catalogues of other academic libraries in Manchester and Salford, and of the

British Library, the Library of Congress, the Bibliotheque Nationale and the National Library of Wales are among the many important research tools. Information and bibliographical searches can be made by computer on request. The Library holds copies of all postgraduate and some undergraduate theses produced in the University. Postgraduate theses are listed by department and author in a card index at the start of the Short Loan Index on the ground floor. Material relevant to women's history is to be found under American Studies, Anthropology, Education, Government, and Sociology as well as History.

The Library has a major European Documentation Centre (Reader Guide GS. 4) with statistical and other information, and a wide-ranging collection of British Government Publications (Guide, GS. 5). There are extensive newspaper holdings of mainly British newspapers (Guide GS. 6); two major cuttings collections, from the *Guardian* and the *Daily Mail*, and a picture library from the *Mail*. The important medical and hospital records are discussed in the separate section on Manchester medical records.

Archives:
1) **Manchester University Archive Collections** (see Reader Guide GS.3). These are essential sources for the history of Manchester University, the history of higher education in general, the development of teaching in various academic disciplines, and the history of student activities. A detailed list of the University's Archives is available at the Ground Floor Information Desk and in the Archives Card Catalogue. The following are of particular interest to those researching the involvement of women in higher education, especially at Manchester University. An article by A. Robertson on women's education at Manchester University is shortly to appear in the *Bulletin*.

a) UA/4/1-24. Material relating to the education of women, including the Women's Department at Owens College (the department was established in 1883); a scrap book compiled by Edith Wilson (the first tutor of women students, 1883-1904) relating to the activities of women students and the women's department; Manchester University Women's Union; Manchester Association for Promoting the Higher Education of Women; Manchester and Salford College for Women; reminiscences of the Women's Department in the 1930s, collected by Mabel Tylecote.

UA/14. Archives of the Manchester University Settlement including annual reports, and the correspondence of Edith Wilson.

UA/16/4. Obituary notice of Mary Hope Hogg (1863-1936), Warden, Ashburne Hall for Women, 1917-1930.

UA/73. Student departmental publications, including the newsletter of the Owens College Department for women, 1887-1894.

b) Registrar's Department: includes staff and student registers, records of staff appointments and material on halls of residence.

c) Vice Chancellor's Archives: correspondence from women including Margaret Ashton, Mary Tout, Julia Varley, Edith Wilson; and from women's organisations including Cheltenham Ladies College, a Home for Gentlewomen (Higher Broughton, Manchester), Manchester High School for Girls (1900-1912), Manchester University Women's Union, National Union of Women Workers, North of England Society for Women's Suffrage, Young Woman's Christian Association.

d) Archives of individuals, mostly academics:
Samuel Alexander, Professor of Philosophy, 1883-1924, woman's suffrage supporter. Papers include correspondence with several prominent women, such as Emilia Dilke, Annie Horniman, Naomi Mitchison,

Eliza Orme, Eleanor Rathbone, Mary Stocks, Marie Stopes, Sybil Thorndike, Beatrice Webb.

T.F. Tout, Professor of Medieval and Modern History, 1890-1925. Papers include political material and extensive correspondence. Tout's female relatives were active in the campaign for women's suffrage. Mary Tout was involved in the University Women's Federation and was first Chair of the Women's Union.

Sir Frederick Maurice Powicke archive contains a few items of interest including a letter from Ellen Wilkinson.

Margaret Pilkington, 1891-1974, curator of the Whitworth Art Gallery.

George Unwin (1870-1921): pioneering Professor of Economic History; his papers include material on Bolton in the 1830s.

Mabel Tylecote collection of an important educationalist and Labour Party figure (1896-1986) [NIDS UK, 0.063.096]

Katherine Tynan Collection (Irish poet and novelist, 1861-1931)

Doris Bailey of the Department of Physics, laboratory notebook from 1911.

Shirley Lerner, lecturer in Industrial Relations, (papers c.1938-1969)

e) Catalogue of portraits, paintings, photographs and busts belonging to the University. Several depict women academics and wardens of halls of residence: examples include Mildred Pope, chair of French Language and Romance Philology, 1934-9; Dr Catherine Chisholm, first woman graduate in medicine and clinical lecturer in children's diseases, 1919-49. There is a complete set of photographs of student groups at Ashburne Hall for women since 1901.

2) **Labour Party Library Collections** include two substantial collections: Labour Party Pamphlets and Reports Collection (LPPRC) and Labour Party Newspaper Cuttings Collection (LPNCC). (See Reader Guide GS.1).

a) LPPRC: some 10,000 pamphlets, reports and other material published mainly between 1900 and 1970 by the Labour Party, and by socialist organisations in other countries, with some government and company reports. Of particular interest are the Labour Party Annual Conference Reports (on microfilm) and pamphlets issued by the Fabian Society, ILP, Socialist League and Clarion Press. Further Fabian and ILP material is available at Deansgate (see separate entry). Hard copy material for a range of political organisations is listed in the main catalogue at Owens. Labour Party publications include a number of pamphlets and leaflets on Labour Party women's organisations, and on issues affecting women and children, especially reports prepared for the National Conferences of Labour Women by the Standing Joint Committee of Industrial Women's Organisations.

b) LPNCC. Volume 1, 1909 -1983, contains some 40,000 envelopes of newspaper cuttings containing over 1 million individual cuttings taken mainly from British, with some from foreign, newspapers. They are arranged by subject heading, including 'women', but references to women will be found throughout. Under 'women' for example can be found cuttings on the Housewives' League, National Council of Women, Open Door Council, 6 Point Group, Townswomen's Guilds, Women's Parliaments; under 'Labour' there is material on equal pay, 1918, and on 'women's labour'; under 'sex relations', material on abortion, divorce.

3) **The (Manchester) Guardian Archives** (see Reader Guide GS.2; handlists can be consulted at the Ground Floor Information Desk). The manuscript archive includes General Correspondence, 1872 -1929, 1932 -1956, and the correspondence of editors C.P. Scott (1872-1929); A.P. Wadsworth (1944 -1956); and H. Alastair Hetherington (1956 - 75). Specific items of interest include letters from women such as Sylvia

Pankhurst and Nancy Astor, material on C.P. Scott's family, Withington High School for Girls, University Scholarships for women (1918-1922), employment of women on the *Guardian* (1938-1959) and copies of *Guardian* articles written by women's page editor, 1955-1968. The archive also contains the records of the *Manchester Evening News.*

4) Records of other societies and organisations.
a) Bolton and District Operative Cotton Spinners' Provincial Association: extensive material on the cotton industry in south- east Lancashire and nearby. Union material includes ledgers, annual reports (1874-1972) and local branch material.
b) Manchester Branch of the Association of University Teachers, c. 1914-1934.

Microform, Audio-visual Material: this is available from the Audio-visual office on the Ground Floor, where lists and guides to microfilm collections are also kept. At the start of the main card catalogue are drawers containing lists of most audio-visual and microform holdings but these are not complete. Other material can be located through the author/title card catalogue (for instance under Labour Party, Conservative Party etc) or through the on-line catalogue accessible by computer. Microform collections include copies of printed books and of archives. There is a collection of 19th century American pamphlets and the Library subscribes to the projects microfilming items in the *Short Title Catalogues* of *Early English Printed Books*, 1475-1640 (Mx 16), *Early English Books,* 1641-1700 (Mx 17), and *The Eighteenth Century* (Mx 45). Ultimately the Library will contain copies of all books published in English before the 19th century.

Important political holdings are available in microform: the Archive of the British Labour Party, Series II, Pamphlets and Leaflets (ref. Mfx 108); Labour Party Annual Conference Reports, 1901-1960 (M 493); the Archives of the British Labour Party, Part I, NEC minutes of the Labour Representative Committee, 1900-1906, and the Labour Party,

1906-67 (Mfx 5); The Archives of the British Conservative and Unionist Party, 1869 -1986 (Mfx 6) with a detailed guide to the collection (329.9422); The Archives of the British Liberal Party, Series I, Pamphlets and Leaflets, 1884 -1974 (Mfx 123). The Archives of the Trades Union Congress, and a British Trade Union History Collection (of pamphlets and other printed material) are also held. There is a microform collection of Irish Political and Radical Newspapers of the Twentieth Century (Mx 27) and a run of *Justice*, the paper of the Social Democratic Federation.

Other important manuscripts from other institutions available in microform include (names of collection and reference number): Charlotte Bronte (M584, M2626); Marie Antoinette Duschene (M2553);Mary Estlin (M316); Elizabeth Gaskell (M341, 351, 357, 584, 2626); Annie Horniman - personal papers and correspondence (Mf 1174 at Owens, and Mf 1177 at Deansgate); International Women's Suffrage Alliance and NUWSS correspondence (M2679/8); Minute Books of the Parliamentary Committee for Women's Suffrage (M2679/2); Correspondence of the Manchester Men's League for Women's Suffrage (M2679/4); papers, political diaries and correspondence of C.P. Scott of *the Manchester Guardian* (M2705); Sylvia Pankhurst Papers, 1882 - 1960 (M2707); Archives of Macmillan and Company, 1856 -1923 (Mx46); Holograph Diary of Beatrice Webb, 1873 -1943 (Mf 685); Papers of the Manchester Statistical Society, 1833 -1843 (Mf 765); Frank Pettingell collection of 19th century English plays (Mx 56); Mass-Observation file reports, 1937-49 (Mfx 110); William Clarke papers - material on the political activities of the English parliamentarian army of the 1640s and 1650s, including material on women prophets; Earls Colne Collection: Records of an English Village 1400 -1750 (Mf 841).

Tapes, films and videos include: recording of Alison Uttley (TRC 23, 24); 'Life before birth' - slides of foetal development compiled by Marjorie A. England, 1985 (SL 66, 67); video-tape of the life of Mary Baker Eddy, of the First Church of Christ (Scientology), 1988 (VCR 102).

The Deansgate Building
John Rylands University Library of Manchester,
150 Deansgate,
Manchester M3 3EH
Tel. 061 834 5343/6765
Sub-Librarian in charge of Deansgate: Dr Peter McNiven, Head of
Special Collections.

Type of Institution: The John Rylands Library was founded by Mrs Enriqueta Rylands in memory of her husband, a Wigan cotton magnate and philanthropist. In 1972 it merged with the Library of Manchester University and now serves as the repository for the University's 'Special Collections': manuscripts, and early or rare printed books along with a variety of reference or associated material. Deansgate's collections are an under-explored treasure trove: as the Library's own guide states, it holds manuscripts in 50 different languages, the oldest dated in the 3rd century B.C.; and printed books from the early 15th century to the present day. There are more than 8,000 English books printed before 1640, 34,500 foreign books earlier than 1601. Most material is on 'closed access': items have to be ordered using the reference numbers from the catalogue.

Access: Open Monday - Friday: 10 am - 5.30pm; Saturday 10 am - 1pm. Disabled access is difficult in this Victorian building, but help can be provided. Admission is by reader's ticket. A Manchester University Library ticket is valid for Deansgate, otherwise you need to write in advance for a ticket. A letter of introduction and proof of identity are normally required. In 1987 the John Rylands Research Institute was established to make the collections better known and to encourage their use: bursaries are available for specialised projects using the Library's holdings.

Catalogues: A good place to start is with the Library's own publications discussed above. Reader Guides GS. 9 is to the 'Deansgate Building'. The 'Prospectus' of the John Rylands Research Institute gives a general introduction to collections. *Bulletin of the John Rylands University Library of Manchester,* volume 71 (2), Summer 1989, contains many useful articles (on English books from the 17th to the 19th centuries; on sources for Protestant nonconformity, for the history of the north-west, for popular culture, for science, technology and medicine). The leaflet, 'Recent and Forthcoming Publications', is useful for the most recent information on the Deansgate collections, as is the *John Rylands Research Institute Newsletter*, issued free of charge in May and November.

For printed books there are three principal author catalogues: one of the Rylands collection in 1899; the second covering accessions between 1899 and 1978; the third of the University's special collections of rare books, with books acquired since 1978. A large subject index relates to the second catalogue and there is a smaller subject index for the third. A card index arranging the original collection chronologically is useful for some types of research. A microfiche version of the catalogues to printed books was produced by Chadwyck-Healey in 1988.

It is impossible to give a complete account of the lists and catalogues available for manuscript material. There are 'Handlists' of 'English manuscripts'; of 'Western manuscripts'; Latin, Spanish, Coptic, Oriental manuscripts and so on, plus a variety of lists of specific collections. The general guides listed above provide a start, and Library staff will help.

All existing published and unpublished guides to the archives in the Library are available on microfiche in the Chadwyck-Healey project, the National Inventory of Documentary Sources in the United Kingdom (known as NIDS UK) which is available in major libraries, including the main University Library. The reference number for Rylands material is 0.063, so, for example, the handlist of 'English manuscripts' published in 1928 is 0.063.007 while the unpublished list of the correspondence of the Legh family of Lyme is 0.063.120. Some of the Library's own collections (including material on suffrage and the Elizabeth Gaskell collection) are available on microfilm (copies are kept at Owens). Details of microfilm are given in the 'Recent and Forthcoming Publications' leaflet.

Collections: Some of Deansgate's vast holdings have not been fully or even partially listed because resources have been scarce and Deansgate's strengths in traditional historical fields are only now becoming fully known. It is hard therefore to do more than indicate briefly the value of the Library for women's studies and feminist research. The collections cover a wide range of themes, times and places but our own expertise has inevitably meant a focus on post-medieval British material.

Periodicals: there is a very rich collection of current periodicals including the publications of local history and religious societies some of which are not held at Owens or the Central Reference Library. There are good runs of older political periodicals including Owenite, Chartist, and ILP material. The E.L. Burney collection includes many women's magazines including a run of *Titbits* for the 1880s. The Library holds *Common Cause* and other suffrage serials.

Printed books: Amongst material of relevance for women's history are important collections of medical books from the 15th to the 18th centuries including many early midwifery texts (catalogues available); much theological material including the Midgely Collection (catalogue available) of early Quaker material which has works by women; ballads, broadsides, chapbooks (including important Irish and Scottish material); several thousand 19th century anti-slavery pamphlets; a large amount of political literature including Fabian Society and Labour Party material collected by Mabel Tylecote; 750 British pamphlets from 1875 -1890; a British Election Literature collection, c. 1931 -1966, covering national and local material, Conservative, Labour, Liberal and minor parties, and independent candidates including Eleanor Rathbone at Liverpool. For the period after 1950 this refers mainly to the Manchester area. There are children's books; collections of novels; an extensive collection of suffrage histories; Jewish literature; French Revolutionary material; music scores and much more.

Manuscripts: Amongst the enormous holdings are several important collections directly concerned with women: the Hester Thrale-Piozzi manuscripts deal with an important literary figure of the late 18th, early 19th centuries; a large collection of Elizabeth Gaskell material includes correspondence and original manuscripts of her books; the Fanny Burney collection includes travel journals, manuscripts of plays and material relating to the actress Sarah Siddons; the Bagshawe papers include Lady Mary Wortley Montagu material; Annie Horniman (1860 -1937) collection includes newspaper cuttings and correspondence of this prominent theatrical woman; the Alison Uttley collection includes manuscripts of her works, correspondence and photographs; there is Mrs G. Linnaeus Banks material in the E.L. Burney collection amongst other material on women's literature; English Manuscripts 1122-1129 are the antiquarian works and travel journals of Dorothy Richardson, a late 18th-century Yorkshirewoman. Pre-Raphaelite material (centred on Holman Hunt and Burne-Jones) and the Ruskin collection includes correspondence by and about women artists and patrons.

Women are important as collectors as well as in the collections: there are the Margaret D. Paton collection of literary papers and the Anna T. Hill collection of modern novels, for example.

There are extensive papers for provincial anti-slavery societies including letters and minutes of the Sheffield Female Anti-Slavery society. Suffrage material includes the records of the Manchester Men's League for Women's Suffrage [NIDS UK 0.063.060]; National Union of Women's Suffrage Society material; Parliamentary Committee for Women's Suffrage; Catholic Women's Suffrage Society; International Women's Suffrage Society. Deansgate holds the records of Accrington Conservative Association, c. 1880 -1966.

The value of family papers was discussed in the introduction and the Deansgate Library has rich holdings, especially for north-west families: Bromley-Davenport, Cornwall-Legh, Legh of Lyme are amongst the major collections. All contain correspondence, diaries, marriage and other settlements, and financial papers, vital for the study of elite women. The Heald papers include (English MS 1218) thirty-one volumes of diaries kept by Emily Isabel Heald, 1869 -1911; the Nicholson papers contain letters concerning the courtship of Elizabeth Seddon and James Nicholson in the 1730s. Furthermore, family papers also have much of value for the study of other social groups: household and estate accounts are useful for women's employment; manorial records held by these families as lords of manors provide insights into social and economic relationships at village level. Local government material such as overseers' of the poor and constables' records is often found within family collections: the Aston of Aston papers, for example, include Health Board material on cholera in Cheshire in the early 1830s.

Material on women in industry is included in the records both of Trade Unions and Employers (eg Oldham Textile Employers' Archives). The manuscript collection of A.P. Wadsworth, editor of the *Manchester Guardian* 1944-56, includes account books of Lancashire cotton manufacturers and more Linnaeus Banks material. The Oldknow Papers (English MS. 751 -840) on the Lancashire cotton industry of the later 18th and early 19th centuries, include as MS 815, a 'Disgrace Account' which details mistakes by women workers, conduct reports, information on wages etc.

The printed books include many religious works by or about women. Besides the Methodist collection described below the Library has extensive manuscript and printed holdings relating to Baptists, Unitarians, Moravians and the Christian Brethren of the 19th and 20th centuries. This last is the largest collection in the world and includes details of the work of female missionaries. The Congregational College Archives 1800 -1970 cover colleges in Lancashire, Yorkshire, Nottingham, Bristol and elsewhere while the William Temple Foundation Archives includes records of William Temple College and of the Industrial Mission Association of Great Britain. Complete records of the Belgian temporalities of the order of the English Canonesses of the Holy Sepulchre, established in 1642, are also held.

The Methodist Archives and Research Centre

The record office and Library of the Methodist Church of Great Britain is located in Deansgate. Opening hours and access arrangements are the same as for the Library as a whole. The Methodist Archivist is Dr Peter Nockles, who should be contacted in advance of any visit.

Catalogues: This is a collection where advice from the archivist is essential. There are extensive catalogues but it is difficult to search such large holdings by topic. A guide produced by the University can be purchased for £1 while material acquired up to 1983-4 is listed in H.L. Calkin, *Catalog of Methodist Archival and Manuscript Collections* part 6 (Arlington, 1985). However, this is not complete and Calkin used his own numbering rather than the Rylands', so individual items still have to be looked up in the Deansgate catalogues. The catalogues are: of the complete printed works of John and Charles Wesley; of periodicals - many unique to the Rylands; a guide to pamphlets, organised by author, title and subject. (These are boxed in date order and for some purposes it is easier to order up a box or two around the date you are interested in.) There is a catalogue of books, including hymnals and histories of methodism, and a card catalogue of manuscripts including approximately 25,000 letters from the 18th and 19th centuries. A guide to official Methodist records, includes records of the Conference and circuits, as well as many non-Wesleyan Methodist records. These do not include registers or other records of local churches.

Some of the handlists are available on microfiche in NIDS UK 0.063. 159-161, 186 -194; and further microform guides are currently being published by the Inter Documentation Company of Leiden, as *The People Called Methodists: A Documentary History of the Methodist Church in Great Britain and Ireland.*

Collections: Missionary magazines and other periodicals are good sources for women's activities in the Church. Personal papers of Methodists include a great deal of information about women's lives.

118

There are letters and diaries, for example, of the Countess of Huntingdon, Hannah Ball, and Hester Anne Roe. The Fletcher-Tooth collection contains much material on everyday life in Madeley in Shropshire in the 18th century. Locating women in some of the institutional records is difficult but there are records of women's activities as preachers in much of the non-Wesleyan material, and there is considerable information about women's charitable and philanthropic activities on a local and a national level.

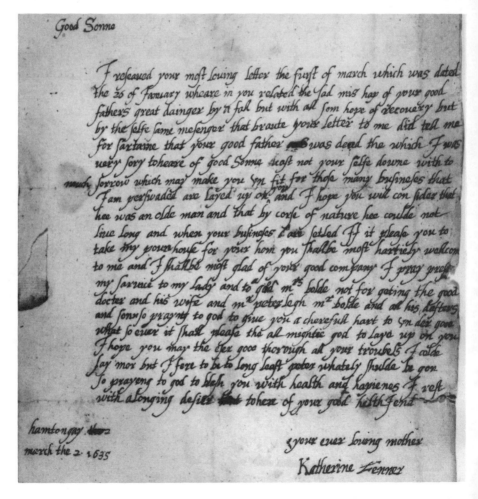

Katherine Fenner to her son-in-law Francis Legh, 2 March 1635. Reproduced by courtesy of the Director and University Librarian, the John Rylands University Library of Manchester.

Saddleworth Museum and Art Gallery
High Street
Uppermill
nr Oldham OL3 6HS
Tel: 0457 874093
Curator: Sue Latimer

Type of Institution: Independent trust run museum situated in an area noted for its historic associations, particularly the Industrial Revolution and the textile industry. This is reflected in the museum's collection of mainly 19th and 20th century local history material such as documents, photographs, and records relating to local firms, workers, societies, schools and families. Saddleworth Historical Society's Archive is also housed in the museum.

Access: The museum is open daily including week-ends and bank holidays. Winter opening hours (November, December, January and February) are 1 - 4pm; Opening hours from March to October are: Monday to Saturday 10am - 5pm; Sundays 12 noon - 5pm. Researchers are welcome, but telephone for an appointment. Limited disabled access: telephone for assistance. Photocopying. Can be reached by bus, road and rail from Manchester and Leeds.

Catalogue: A card index system is arranged by provenance (donation) and subject. Each item is catalogued by letter and number. A photocopy of both the Museum and Historical Society index can be consulted at Oldham Local History Library.

Collections:
Employment and trade union records: Records of the Amalgamated Weavers' Approved Society (c. 1920 -) including a political section minute book. Labour certificates belonging to local women workers (late 19th, early 20th century). Also, birth certificate for Hannah Swarbrick, issued to comply with the Factory and Workshops Act of 1901. Housewife's certificate issued to Sarah Miller by Marple Urban District council in 1906, plus her Labour certificates. Copy of Anne

Chadderton, 'The Early Days of Saddleworth Weavers' Union. Photographs of women in mills, tending looms, etc.

Health records: Minutes of the Uppermill and District Nursing Association (1925-1939). Copy of the Rules of the General Nursing Council for England and Wales (1924). Manual for Hospital Nurses (1878). Circular of discharge of Sarah Taylor from Manchester Infirmary (1798). Household remedy manuals, e.g. *Women's Ailments* (n.d.)

Society records: Rule book of the United Females Friendly Society (1856). Friarmere Relief Fund Book (1862-63), plus minutes of committee meetings.

Poor Law records: Documents relating to Saddleworth Board of Guardians include a receipt for an Assistant Matron's salary (1866), a workhouse letter book, photograph of Saddleworth Assessment Committee, Saddleworth Guardians' Yearbooks (1908-27), and a *History of Saddleworth Workhouse* (1987) by T. Eckersley.

Family and personal papers: Transcript of tapes with Mrs H. Sutcliffe, the daughter of Lord Rhodes, plus other information on the Rhodes family. Documents and photographs relating to local families, e.g. the Buckleys of Tunstead, the Wood Family (early 20th century), letters from American immigrants John and Mary Denton to relatives in Saddleworth (1873). Letters from the author Phyllis Bentley (1938).

Wartime records: Red Cross Society badges and certificates (World Wars 1 and II). Extensive collection of World War II material - e.g. Ministry of Information booklet 'Make do and Mend' (1943), ration books, records of a 'Busy Bees' group - knitters of scarves, etc. for servicemen. World War 1 photographs of medical and housing staff at Ashway Gap.

Local history material: good collection of local newspapers, songs and poems. Documents and photographs relating to local schools (some 19th century). Photographs of women on Whit walks, by their shop fronts, in mills, etc.

Salford Art Gallery
Peel Park
Salford, M5 4WU
Tel: 061 736 2649
Museum Officer, Fine and Applied Art: Judith Sandling

Type of Institution: Local authority art gallery, part of the City of Salford Art Gallery and Museums which also includes Salford Museum, Ordsall Hall Museum and the Mining Museum (see separate entry).

Access: Hours are Monday to Friday 10am - 4.45pm, Sunday 2pm - 5pm. The Art Gallery shares the same building as Salford Local History Library and with the museum forms part of Peel Park. It can be reached by car on the A6, with parking in front of the building; by rail to Salford Crescent from Victoria and Piccadilly stations; from Piccadilly bus station - 64, 66, 67, 68 and others. Disabled access to the whole building including the cafe and disabled toilets. To see works in store please telephone for an appointment.

Catalogue: There are no catalogues relating to women artists, but the museum officer for fine and applied art has compiled a list of women artists represented in the collections.

Collection: The art gallery's collections contain a number of works created by women artists. To date there are fifty-six oils and acrylics, including paintings by Eileen Agar, Jadwiga Lutyen Behnisch, Vanessa Bell, Susan Isabel Dacre and Helen Bradley; forty-four drawings and watercolours including the work of Kate Greenaway, Frances Hodgkins, Therese Lessore and Kathleen Walne; fourteen prints some by Elizabeth Frink; three sculptures (one by Frink); photographs by Ruth Blanch and a collage by Daneila Weate. There are many images of women painted by men (e.g. L. S. Lowry) throughout the collection.

The decorative arts collection contains a few pieces by women potters/ artists, such as Gladys Rogers, Suzy Cooper and Clarice Cliffe.

For information about Salford Museum contact the museum officer for social history, Cindy Shaw (tel: 061 736 2649).

Salford City Archives
The Archives Centre
658/662 Liverpool Road
Irlam, Manchester M30 5AD
Tel: 061 775 5643
Archivist: Andrew Cross

Type of Institution: Local authority archives for the area of of Salford, Eccles, Swinton, Pendlebury, Irlam and Worsley, housed in a former police station. Records are mainly concerned with local government affairs and are particularly good for historians.interested in women's involvement in poor law relief and education in the 19th and 20th centuries. There are some family papers of interest and records of local women's organisations, including the Electrical Association for Women and the Soroptimist Club.

Access: Open 9 am - 4.30 pm, Monday to Friday, by arrangement. It is situated on bus routes nos. 10, 11 and 67 and is close to Irlam railway station. There is parking space at the rear of the Centre. Disabled access very difficult. The Archivist is welcoming and helpful.

Catalogue: There are subject, places and persons indexes and a series of catalogues of deposits in the search room, copies of which are available in Salford Local History Library, Salford University Library, GMC Record Office and the Royal Commission on Historical Manuscripts in London. Catalogue references should be quoted in any enquiry. Useful guides include: *A Select Gazetteer of Local Government Areas for Greater Manchester County,* 1982 and *Genealogical Sources for Salford Metropolitan District,* first issued in 1977 and updated every one or two years.

Collections:
Local Government records: Salford Poor Law Union Records (mainly late 19th, early 20th century) - Board of Guardian minutes (1838-1930 incomplete), minutes for the Ladies' Committee (1921-22),

Infirmary Visiting Committee (1882-1912), Workhouse Visiting Committee, Hospital Committee, Children's Committee, Relief Committee, General Purposes Committee, Old People's Homes - Management Committee (various years between 1865 and 1930).

Worsley Township records: Overseers of the Poor, details of membership of sick clubs by pregnant women to prevent their removal from the parish (1795-1829), filiation (maintenance) orders for illegitimate children (1694-1808), bastardy orders and apprenticeship indentures for pauper children (e.g. as girl servants) (1695-1834).

Education records: Chief items of interest are the records of local schools - log books, admission records - particularly good for the pioneer stage of state education (1870 - c.1900), and WW2. Log books recorded events out of the ordinary; they showed the activities of schoolmistresses and their concern for pupils. There is a good collection of records for girls' industrial schools.
Examples: St Mathias School (girls) - log book (1863-97). Evening School for Girls, Tootal Road (probably working girls) (1906-31) - log books. Pendleton High School for Girls - minutes of Governors' meetings (1911-21), list of acceptances for the post of Governor with the Pendleton Trust of the Manchester High School for Girls Foundation (1911-1919, 1927, 1929), and admission details of pupils, such as family background.

Organisation and society records: Eccles and District branch of the Electrical Association for Women (1938-1980) - a national consumer organisation instructing women on how to use electricity. Salford Soroptimist Club (1948-69). Eccles Amateur Dramatic and Operatic Society.

Family papers: Examples include 18th century deeds concerning women's ownership of property in Manchester and Salford; wills of 19th century women; correspondence and photographs of Effie Hirst of Doncaster and Margate, teacher of the deaf.

Photographs: There are two important collections: the S. L. Coulthurst collection - street scenes of Salford in the 1890s, showing women shopping, as market sellers, customers, barmaids and cafe waitresses. The Frank Mullineux collection consists of scenic photos of the Worsley area in the 20th century.

═══════════

Salford Local History Library
Peel Park
Salford M5 4WU
Tel: 061 736 2649
Local History Librarian: Tim Ashworth
Assistant Librarian: Tony Frankland

Type of Institution: Public municipal library, which (since local authority reorganisation in 1974) contains the holdings of three constituent local history libraries: Salford, Swinton, and Eccles. The Library is housed on the ground floor of the Art Gallery built in the 1870s, and is situated within the public gardens of Peel Park. The emphasis is on 19th and 20th century material: local government printed records, books, newspapers, maps and photographs.

Access: Hours are Monday, Tuesday, Thursday and Friday, 10am - 5pm; Wednesday 10am -9pm. Nó prior appointment is needed although it is advisable to book a micro-reader in advance. Staff are helpful to beginners and experienced researchers alike. Disabled access to all parts of the building including a cafe. Photocopying is available. The Library can be reached by public transport (see entry for Salford Art Gallery), and there is free car parking in front of the building.

Catalogue: There are three different catalogues for material housed separately in Salford, Swinton, and Eccles libraries up to 1974, and one catalogue for material received after that date. The card catalogue is divided into author/title, subject and biographical indexes. All material is on open shelf. The Library has its own excellent and detailed information guide, and useful fact sheets and leaflets which cover a wide range of topics such as genealogical records, newspapers and Swinton industrial schools. The following pamphlets are on sale: Emily Glencross, *Breakfast at Windsor, Memories of a Salford Childhood 1914 -28;* Elsie Osman, *For the Love of Ada and Salford;* Barbara Vaughan, *Growing Up in Salford 1918 -28.*

Many of the references in the catalogue are to specific items in books and newspapers, and the researcher is therefore saved time and effort if prepared to explore the catalogue fully. Although there are few items listed under 'women', there is much of interest under other headings such as:
'Labour': Mrs Annot Robinson, 'Substituted Labour of Women, 1914 -17', (Mss 1917-18).
'Strikes': as reference is not always made to the gender of workers on the index card, it is helpful to know whether women were likely to have worked in a particular trade. This is illustrated by the following examples from newspapers: over 1,000 flax workers on strike in 1890 at Adelphi Flax Mill, Salford; twelve mill girls on strike in Salford in 1873 are prosecuted by their employers.
'Prison': appointment of Miss Lord as Matron of New Bailey Prison, Salford, 1830 (source: *Manchester Guardian*).

Collections:
Local history material: The emphasis is on printed material, local government records, books and newspapers. As almost all of the Library's stock is on open shelf, the researcher has the luxury of being able to browse and 'discover'. The collection consists of local government records, such as council minutes from the late 19th century for Salford, Swinton and Pendleton, electoral rolls, census returns, the Roll Call Annual of Swinton, directories for Manchester and Salford (1772 -1969), parish registers and Methodist church records. The Library has an excellent collection of local histories, e.g. *History of Wesleyan*

Methodism in Swinton, and what seem to be general histories at first glance can also hold information about women - for example, Fancher, *Manchester in 1844*, contains statistics on prostitution. There are a number of journals and society periodicals such as a full run of the *Transactions of the Lancashire and Cheshire Antiquarian Society* from 1883. Newspapers are predominantly 19th and 20th century titles, e.g *.Salford Reporter* (indexed), *Swinton Local Journal* from 1874, and *Eccles and Patricroft Journal* from 1874 (partial index).

Photographs: These are arranged according to subject: women and girls on Whit Walks, in school, at work, as shopworkers, walking in parks and campaigning for women's suffrage. A few date back to 1855. Copies are lent to schools and reminiscence aid projects.

Poor Law records: These include 18th century bastardy orders, removal and resettlement orders (1699 -1814), a weekly pay book for relief of the poor in Salford (1756-1779), Salford Guardian Year Books (1924-5), a list of persons receiving poor relief from the Overseers of the Poor in Pendleton (1818) (poster file), report on the aged poor (1895-6), Boarding Out System (Mss 1872-73), workhouse food allowances (Mss 1888-9), newscuttings in the Brotherton Scrapbooks, early 19th century, and E.H. Inchley, *The Work of the Guardians, What is being Done in Salford,* (1926).

School Records and Newspaper References: Examples include a diagram of the system of continuation schools for women and girls (Mss 1895-6), 'The Work of the Manchester School Board' (Mss 1873-4), the Manchester Girls' Institute (*Manchester Faces and Places*, vol 10), Miss Thomasson's seminary for young ladies (*Manchester Guardian*, 1832), St Peter's Church of England Girls' School, log book (1864-1933), Salford Evening School for Girls, log book (1905 -41).

Church records: There are numerous histories, newscuttings, etc, about local churches, chapels and related activities such as the Church Girls' Brigade. Other items of interest include the parochial magazine of St Clement's Church, Broughton (1896-98, 1903) with references to Sunday Schools, the Temperance Society, the Mutual Improvement Society, a ladies' sewing class and the Mothers' Union; an indexed extract of marriages from the Register of Sacred Trinity Church, Salford (1635-1751); and Reports of the Manchester and Salford Society for Promoting Christian Knowledge (1824, 1841 -).

Hospitals: There are references to the Clinical Hospital for Women and Children in *Manchester Faces and Places*, vol 10, and various references to lying-in hospitals and dispensaries for women and children in the 19th century in the *Manchester Guardian*. See also John Hare, 'Salford Hospitals: A Brief History', (1985).

Politics: Apart from a few items such as a circular letter from the Women's Liberal Association in Charlestown in 1944, and a pamphlet of a Communist Party meeting in Pendleton in 1933, the local press is the main source of information. Examples include a report of the opening of a Primrose League branch in Broughton (*Salford Reporter*, 1891), accounts of the Social Democratic Federation, Salford branch, reports of women's suffrage local branch activity c. 1880. See also J.B. Smethurst, 'The Suffragette Movement in Eccles' in Eccles and District History Society, Annual Lectures 1971-2.

Brotherton Scrapbook: These consist of newscuttings (c. 48 volumes) culled from the local press about events and issues of public interest, collected by Joseph and Martha Brotherton, in the (1820s-1850s). Joseph was the first M.P. for Salford and Martha wrote the first vegetarian cookery book; they were active members of the Swedenborgian Church.

Salford Mining Museum
Buile Hill Park
Eccles Old Road
Salford M6 8GL
Tel: 061736 1832
Museum Officer: Alan Davies

Type of Institution: Local authority museum and reference library. The museum is divided into several sections: reconstructions of mine workings, a gallery of mining art, and a display showing the history of coalmining. The library consists of a reference section, archive and object store, and contains material relevant to the history and process of mining: printed and manuscript sources, newscuttings, photographs and artifacts.

Access: Hours are Monday to Friday 10am - 12.30pm, 1.30pm - 5pm; Sunday 2pm - 5pm (museum visitors only). Researchers are welcome, but telephone for an appointment. No disabled access. Photocopying available.

Catalogue: The catalogue is a card index system with material classified by donor, subject and colliery object. Uncatalogued material is also accessible, and there is an accessions register.

Collection: The library of 15,000 volumes holds a variety of material relating to the social and labour history of mining and its processes, including statistical information and government reports. Much of the collection pertains to the North West, but it also includes items relating to the rest of Britain and abroad. Of particular interest to historians of women are the following:

Archival material: Looseleaf folder labelled 'Miscellaneous/Colliery Girls' (U 263/Z 29) containing notes and newscuttings about pit-brow women (1879-1982), a photographic copy of a painting of a pit brow lassie (n.d.), letters from the historian Angela V. John relating to pit-brow women, and a reprint of her article in the *Bulletin of the John Rylands University Library* , 'Colliery legislation and its consequences:

1842 and the women miners of Lancashire' 1978. Miscellaneous collection of publications of research on pit-brow women in this country and abroad (for example, publications held in the German Museum of Mining). There are also reports of Government committees and commissions into the mining industry in the 19th and 20th centuries such as the Children's Employment Commission (1842) which describes women and children's working conditions below ground.

Photographs and Illustrations: The library has a large photographic collection depicting collieries and side branches of the industry which includes images of women working at collieries, a small collection of old postcards depicting women in the Wigan area, and a good selection of illustrations published in Victorian magazines, e.g. pit brow women depicted in the *Illustrated London News* and *The Graphic*. The museum also has catalogues of exhibitions, and a few artifacts of interest such as a pair of pit-brow clogs and a human harness, possibly worn by a woman working underground in the 19th century.

University of Salford Library
Salford M5 4WT
Tel: 061 745 5000 (main switchboard)
Director and University Librarian: Dr C.G.S. Harris

Type of Institution: University undergraduate and research library. Salford Technical Institute was founded in 1896; it became a College of Advanced Technology in 1956 and a University in 1967. In 1961 non-advanced work was transferred to Salford Technical College (now University College Salford).

Access: Researchers should apply to the Librarian in advance for permission to consult Special Collections. The Special Collections Room is on the second floor of the Library; disabled access. Open: weekdays 9am -9pm; Saturday 9am -12 noon, in term; more restricted hours in vacation.

Catalogue: There is a computerized catalogue for the Library's main holdings. For the archives and other special collections, Library Leaflet 11 (Special Collections) is a brief introductory guide which directs researchers to other lists and finding aids.

Collections: The main Library collections include small but expanding holdings of books and periodicals on women and gender (an M.A. in Women's Studies has recently been set up). Special collections with some potential for women's history include General and Local Election Pamphlets and Publicity Material, 1950-1974 (including posters and broadsheets); family papers of the Duke of Bridgewater (the Canal Duke) including correspondence of female family members, late-18th and early 19th centuries; manuscripts and correspondence of local authors Walter Greenwood (*Love on the Dole*) and Stanley Houghton (*Hindle Wakes*). The collections covering the University's own history may be useful for the history of women's education. The Registrar's Department keeps a working archive while the University Library's 'Local Collection' comprises press cuttings (about 30,000 items) and departmental publications (about 25,000 items). The press cuttings range from national coverage of the University as an institution to stories in local papers about individual students. The departmental papers include student newspapers among the published material, notices, memoranda etc. A photographic archive covers the history of the institution since the 1890s, including buildings, teaching sessions, honorary degree ceremonies etc. One picture shows Ellen Wilkinson as Minister of Education speaking at the College in 1946.

Stockport Archives and Local Studies Collection
Central Library,
Wellington Road South,
Stockport SK1 3RS
Tel. 061474 4530
Archivist: Margaret Myerscough
Senior Library Assistant: Ros Lathbury

Type of Institution: Archives and Local Studies material in Study Room of Central library. It contains the records of the public authorities that made up the 1974 metropolitan borough of Stockport, a variety of private and institutional material, and printed local sources. The Study Room and the adjoining Information Room also contain useful reference material, on open access.

Access: Open Mon. - Fri. 9am - 8pm, except Wed. 10am - 8pm; Sat. 9am - 4pm. Disabled access: the Study Room is on the first floor but a stairlift is provided. The Archivist is available 9am - 5pm weekdays, and advance notice is advisable for consultation of archives outside these hours. Archives and specialised local history material have to be requested at the desk.

Catalogue: The library has produced a series of Local Studies Handlists, one of which is an introduction to the archives, divided into Official Records (pertaining to the current area of Stockport Borough) and Unofficial Records (private, business, and organisation records). There are more detailed Calendars of Archives along with lists of recent accessions and uncalendared material at the Inquiry Desk. Other indexes there cover newspapers, microform material, photographs (including the heading 'women') while there is a subject, author and title index to the Local Studies material. The subject index has such headings as 'strikes', 'hatting', 'women in sport'. Staff are very helpful in guiding researchers to relevant material. General reference material is included in the main computer catalogue for all Stockport's holdings.

Collections:

Official records for the townships, urban and rural district councils that are now part of Stockport Metropolitan Borough as well as material for the old Borough of Stockport. Areas covered include Bredbury and Romily, Heaton Norris, Reddish, Cheadle and Gatley, Offerton, Hazel Grove and Bramhall, and Marple. Most of the material dates from the 19th century (although there are 18th century poor law records for Stockport). Records include minutes of councils and committees: for Stockport gas, town hall, tramways, 19th century; wage records from schools, baths, wash houses, highways, sewers, hospitals, etc, mostly 20th century; maternity and child welfare committee, (1918 -1937); school board material and school records (teachers 1898-1958, higher education 1907-9, employment of children 1944-58, individual schools' log books, and records of the children's home and youth club founded in 1941 by Olive Kenyon); medical officer of health material; police daily report sheets 1930-38; manor court records, dating from the 15th century, but mostly 19th century; poor law records from 1837 (workhouse inmates 1842-3, accounts 1887-92, relief lists 1854, rate books).

Unofficial records include:
Estate and family papers, e.g.: Mottram (hatter-grocer) and Harris (cotton spinner) papers 1811-1970; Legh of Lyme accounts 1727-1806; Miss K.M.H. Sidebottom's papers including a family magazine of 1869-76 compiled by young gentlewomen and travel diaries 1879-1907; papers of nurse Margaret Wheatcroft 1903-5; recipe book and postcards of Miss Cheetham, 19th and 20th centuries.
Business and trade papers, e.g.: Christy and Co Hat Manufacturers 1612-1974; Isaac Pearson Ltd cotton spinners, including wage ledgers 1903-6; Cooperative Society's Reddish Confectionery Works 1940s and 50s.
Institutions and societies, e.g.: Standing Conference of Women's Organisations minutes, 1944-82; Certified Assistant Teachers/Class Teachers Association, 1902-47; National Union of Teachers district associations, 1877-1974; Sunday School deeds, minutes, accounts, correspondence, mostly 19th century; accounts and registers of many Methodist churches and the Unitarian church in Stockport 1719-1964; Maternity and Child Welfare Voluntary Committee 1914-86; Chinley

and Bugsworth Women's Liberal Association; Stockport Labour Church 1909 -1932; Stockport Labour Party, 1921 -1969; Stockport Liberal Association, 1868 -1949; Stockport Reform Club, 1888 - 1960.

Local studies material: includes printed minutes, annual reports and publications of local councils, and organisations; a comprehensive collection of local directories; local histories and the publications of local record and historical societies. Some theses on Stockport are available. Much material is to be consulted on microfilm: Land Tax Records, electoral registers, parish registers (for Cheadle and Stockport from the 16th century, Marple from the 17th, besides more recent, including Nonconformist material); census returns, burgess lists for Stockport borough; and newspapers. There are copies of the *Manchester Mercury*, 1752-1830, of the *Stockport Advertiser* and other local papers from the 1820s onwards, as well as Cheshire titles and the *Times* and *Guardian*.

The library has a small number of uncatalogued oral history tapes, mostly connected to its published life histories. These are available for purchase from the library and include. Elizabeth Thompson: *One Child's War*, and Maureen Bell, *Portwood Girl*. Details of the tapes, and arrangements for consulting them are available on application to the library. Most photographs are of buildings, but folders of photocopies of some topics, including women's work are available. Other folders cover Industry (including many wartime photos), Work (including the women's workhouse), Leisure (religious outings, parades, etc) and Weddings. General reference material includes, in the Study Room, Guides to other libraries including neighbouring local record offices and the Public Record Office, the *Wellesley Index to Victorian Periodicals*, and so on. The Information Room holds current periodicals and biographical dictionaries, such as Janet Leggett, *Local Heroines: A Women's History Gazetteer to England, Scotland and Wales* (1988).

Tameside Local Studies Library
Astley Cheetham Public Library,
Trinity Street,
Stalybridge, SK15 2BN
Tel. 061 338 2708/3831
Local History Librarian: Alice Lock. Archivist: Gillian Cooke

Type of Institution: Public library and archives office for the post-1974 Metropolitan Borough of Tameside which incorporates the old towns of Ashton-under-Lyne, Audenshaw, Denton, Droylsden, Dukinfield, Hyde, Longdendale, Mossley, and Stalybridge. It is in Stalybridge town centre, within walking distance of the bus and railway stations. It contains much printed, manuscript, photographic and oral history material of interest to historians of women; staff are very aware of the material's potential for women's history, and very encouraging to researchers. Books, prints and greeting cards from the area are for sale; and the library also offers slide packs and exhibitions for loan. Slide packs include 'The Women's Suffrage Movement in the North West'; and 'Mary Moffat of Kuruman', a missionary born in Dukinfield in 1795. The Local Studies Library encourages donations or loans of local material and librarians are anxious that records of women's organisations and of individuals should be preserved for future generations. (Public access to material can be restricted if necessary.)

Access: Open 9 am - 7.30pm, Monday - Friday and 9.am - 4pm Saturday. Closed Thursday. All researchers welcome. Wheelchair access very difficult. Advanced booking is necessary to reserve a microfilm reader and to order some manuscript material (especially local authority archives) kept in storage.

Catalogue: There is a card index for printed material organised by author, subject and classification number; the heading women points towards some material on suffrage, welfare, work and organisations. Separate indexes are provided for oral history tapes (by name and subject); sound recordings (by performer); framed photographs (by subject); and Broadsides (author and title). There are partial indexes for the *North Cheshire Herald* and *Hyde Reporter*. The library produces an invaluable guide to printed material, *Tameside Bibliography* (1992); there are sections on women's history, autobiographies, public health, trade unionism and the labour movement, Chartism, hatting, and so on. For archives there is a summary *Guide to Records Collection* which can be followed up with more detailed lists. There is also an integrated card index incorporating name, place and subject; women is not a useful heading here. A leaflet *Family History at Tameside Local Studies Library* surveys the sources and methods for family history.

Collections:

Manuscript material: There are voluminous **local government records** of the townships, local boards and urban district councils that made up the 1974 borough. They date mostly from the 19th century and include minutes, rate books and poor law material (here there are some 18th century records). Townships represented are Ashton, Audenshaw, Denton, Dukinfield, Haughton, Hyde, Hollingworth, Mottram, Newton, Mossley, Staley, Werneth. Urban District Councils covered are Audenshaw, Denton, Droylsden, Dukinfield, Hollingworth, Longdendale, Mossley, Mottram, Stalybridge, Ashton and Hyde.
There are records of Maternity and Child Welfare Committees for Ashton (1940 -48), and Hyde (1916 -35).
There are some school board records and fuller material for 20th century Education Committees, along with sources for individual schools and colleges including several Mechanics Institutes and the Ashton Women's Institute and Commercial School for Girls.

Hospital records include patient, staff and committee records for Ashton-under-Lyne Infirmary, 19th and 20th centuries (DD/H/1); late 19th and 20th century material for Hyde Isolation Hospital (DD/H/2); and records for Aspland Maternity Home, 1920s and 1930s (DD/H/3). (There are restrictions on access for many hospital records).

Church records include some parochial material for the Church of England (17th century onwards) and rich holdings for Nonconformist congregations including utopian 19th century churches such as the Christian Israelites as well as Baptist and Methodist records.

labour movement and political records include correspondence and minutes for Stalybridge and Hyde Constituency Labour Party, 1950 -74 (ref DD 55); and for Ashton Labour Party, 1937 -1965 (DD 88); minutes, accounts and correspondence for Ashton and District Trades Council (DDTC); and the records of many individual unions. Material survives for the Cotton Famine Relief Committees of Hyde (DD120, 1862 -1865) and Droylsden (DD173, 1862 -1893).

Society records of relevance to women's history include:

(DD18): A minute book (1909-18) and other records of the Ashton Branch of the North of England Society for Women's Suffrage.

(DD19): Records of the Droylsden Sick Nursing Association, 1892 - 1924, one of the many public health organisations run mainly by women.

(DD75):Minutes of the Ashton Citizens Advice Bureau, another organisation run largely by women, 1940 -1946.

(DD284): Records of Buckton Vale Townswomen's Guild 1899- 1985.

(DD16): Records of the Hyde Students Association: an early 20th century voluntary society devoted to cultural activities involving men and women 1892 -1937.

Business and family papers include those for the Clarke family (ref. DDI), major landowners in the Hyde area in the 19th century, while the letters and accounts of the Lees family of Park Bridge Ironworks (DDL), include much correspondence concerning female members of the family (mid-19th to early 20th centuries) and provide a particularly interesting example of the control of family finances by the male head of household. (See also H. Lees, *The Lees Family of Hazlehurst and Park Bridge,* typescript, 1952. Hannah Lees and sons Ltd was a long established Ashton Ironworks.) Records survive for several 19th and 20th century mills: those for Fletcher's Mill, Ashton, (DDFM), include wages and letter books.

Clarke family papers(DD113) are mid-20th century documents from a working class Ashton couple.

There are several manuscript deposits from individual women, such as the first world war reminiscences of Dorothy Turner (DD131), and (DD237), pamphlets relating to women and health written by Mrs Dowson, an active campaigner on health matters in Hyde in the early 20th century.

Manuscripts left by men also, of course, offer insights into family life: (DD66) writings by Aaron Woollacott, 1850s and 60s, a Swedenborgian preacher, and (DD86) Diaries of James Knight, 1856-62, a Stalybridge school teacher, are examples.

Material on women and war is included in (DD22), letters received by Mossley Women's Voluntary Service, from servicemen during the second world war and (DD103-4): First world war photographs and postcards. There are extensive holdings of local **newspapers**, mostly to be consulted on microfilm; they include *Ashton Reporter, Denton Reporter, Hyde Reporter, Stalybridge Reporter; North Cheshire Herald; Workman's Times,* 1891-3; *Cotton Factory Times,* 1885-1937.

Other material available on microfilm includes census returns for all towns now in Tameside, 1841 -1891; parish registers for Anglican and Nonconformist churches (including much Moravian material); Protestation and Hearth Tax records for the population and social history of the area in the 17th century.

Oral History Collection: There are over 150 tapes recording interviews with women and men who lived and worked in the Tameside area in the early 20th century. Transcripts of the tapes are available on open shelves.

Manchester Studies Tapes are stored at Tameside Local History Library (see separate entry).

Photographic collection: some 30,000 items date from the mid 19th century and include as subjects mills, factories, church activities, shops, markets, schools, Labour organisations such as Hyde Labour Church, strikes. There are also postcards of local views.

Printed Material: The library holds a comprehensive collection of printed local histories, directories, reference works, local record society publications and some general history journals, newscuttings, pamphlets, reports of local organisations (such as Tameside Council for Racial Equality and local union branches), broadsides and maps. Most is on open access, including xeroxes of the broadsides (which range from election addresses to ballads about local women murderers of the 19th century). *The Tameside Bibliography* directs readers to useful secondary sources on women's history relating to the north-west (e.g. Rickie Burman, 'The Jewish women as breadwinner: the changing value of women's work in a Manchester immigrant community', *Oral History*, vol. 10, 2, (Autumn 1982), pp 27 -39; D. Pancott, *A Woman's Place* (a calendar for 1985 illustrated by scenes of Tameside women at work)); and to the library's **biographies and autobiographies** of women who lived in the North-West. Examples include well known material such as Stella Davies, *North Country Bred: a working class family chronicle* (1963) and Hannah Mitchell, *The Hard Way Up* (1977) as well as less familiar material like A. Hindley, *Life in the tent, or travels in the desert and Syria in 1850* (1850) (written by the daughter of Ashton's MP in the 1830s and 1840s); Lilian Slater, *"Think On" Said Mam. Life in Bradford Manchester, 1911 -1919* (1984); E. Weeton, *Miss Weeton's diary of a governess* 1807 - 1825, (2 volumes, first published 1939).

Tameside Museum and Art Gallery Service
Portland Basin Heritage Centre,
1 Portland Place,Portland Street South,
Ashton-under-Lyne, OL6 7SY
Museums Officer: 061 308 3374

Tameside has a wide-ranging museum collection illustrating the social and industrial history of the area. Many items are displayed at Portland Basin Industrial Heritage Centre. The Museums Service is also responsible for a) The Museum of the Manchesters - a social and regimental history, at Ashton Town Hall; b) Astley Cheetham Art Gallery, Stalybridge. Objects from the collection can be loaned or viewed for specific research, exhibition and education purposes. For further information contact the museums officer.

Trafford Borough Libraries Local History Collections

Sale Library (Trafford Local Studies Centre)
Tatton Road, Sale M33 1YH / Tel: 061-872 2101 ex3458
Librarian: Nancy Beals
Open Mon, Tues, Thurs 9am - 7:30pm; Wed, Fri 9am - 5 pm;
Sat 9am - 4pm

Altrincham Library
Stamford New Road, Altrincham WA14 / Tel: 061-928 0317
Librarian: Val Freeman
Open Mon, Tues, Thurs 9am - 7:30pm; Wed, Sat 9am - 4pm;
Fri 9am - 5pm.

Stretford Library
Kingsway, Stretford M32 / Tel: 061-865 2218
Librarian: Mr Newton
Open Mon, Tues, Thurs 9am - 7:30pm; Wed, Sat 9am - 4pm;
Fri 9am - 5pm.

Urmston Library
Crofts Bank Road, Urmston M31 1TZ/ Tel: 061-748 0774
Librarian: Janet Stewart
Open Mon, Fri 9am - 7:30pm; Tues, Wed, Thurs 9am - 5pm;
Sat 9am - 4pm

Type of Institution: Public libraries with local history collections of public and civic material, local newspapers, photographs, and printed records of local organisations. The current borough of Trafford was created out of the formerly independent towns above, and the smaller townships adjacent.

Access: Hours as above. Disabled access varies; contact library.

Catalogue: Because these are local history collections rather than archives, their catalogues do not distinguish between primary and secondary material. All material is catalogued by Dewey number, and not by subject name, but the collections are small enough to browse and the librarians are helpful.

Collection: Sale, as the Local Studies Centre, maintains the largest collection relating to all four towns, including books, maps, pamphlets, press cuttings, rate books, photographs, etc. It has copies of some of the material held in the other three locations. It also has records on microfiche and microfilm relating to the whole borough, including newspapers, census, voter lists, business directories and parish registers. In other words, public or civic records are held here. But private family papers and business records are now in the Greater Manchester Archives.

Sale has begun a 'Places/Events/Subjects' catalogue, which includes a heading for 'Women'. Under this heading are local newspaper articles about groups as diverse as the Women's International League for Peace and Freedom in the 1940s, the Council of Women's Organisations and the Women's Voluntary Service from the 1950s to the 1970s, and the Working Mothers Group in the 1970s. Many of these entries look intriguing -- such as a debate in the 'Sale Pioneer' of 1949 on a resolution demanding the legal right for every wife to compel her husband to share equally the home and income! The sociology numbers (300s) are a place to start in the Dewey catalogue, but a quick flick in the other numbers turned up day nurseries from the 1940s, local poetesses, a report of Sale women's visit to Greenham Common, books of dialect, 19th century housekeepers' account books, and the late 18th century cookery/housekeeping books of Elizabeth Raffald, resident in Stockport and Manchester.

Sale also holds antiquarian serials like those of the Antiquarian Society of Lancashire and Cheshire, Chetham's Society, and the Lancashire and Cheshire Historical Society. And it has the International Genealogical Index for all of Britain, in contrast to the Central Reference Library which holds only that section of the IGI relating to Greater Manchester.

Altrincham, Stretford and Urmston each have local history rooms with local maps, newpaper cuttings, electoral rolls, rates books, house lists, pamphlets (on theatres, schools, churches, soup kitchens, etc), as well as published histories of the area and some antiquarian serials collections. Each also has a collection of photographs. These are largely of streets and buildings, but also of pageants, church outings, societies, libraries, schools, factories, and sewage systems. Stretford also has a local history society collection including oral history tapes and interview transcripts -- of, among other people, the Rose Queen of 1911. Urmston plans future oral history interviews.

Librarians from all four libraries give talks and slide shows on local history to local schools and societies.

Stretford Rose Queen, 1910, courtesy of Stretford Library.

University of Manchester Institute of Science and Technology.
(UMIST)
Sackville Street, Manchester M60
Tel: 061 200 3330
Librarian: P.J. Short Archivist: Mr J. Marsh (see access).

Type of Institution: Faculty of Technology of the University of Manchester from 1904, operating virtually as a separate institution. It was founded as the Manchester Mechanics Institution in 1824 and developed into Manchester Municipal Technical School (1892). This included Schools of Art and Design, Applied Science and Commerce; women attended day and evening classes.

Access: For access to archives application should be made to the Archivist, Mr J. Marsh, c/o Pure and Applied Physics Department, UMIST, PO Box 88, Manchester M60 1QD. (Tel: 061 200 3947/8). The archives are stored in a basement with no disabled access. For access to the Library and its rare books room application should be made to the Librarian. The Library is open 9 am - 8.45 pm weekdays, 9 am - 11.45 am Saturdays in term time; restricted hours in vacations.

Catalogue: There is no catalogue for the archives - the Archivist will supply information. Library books are catalogued by author.

Collections: The main library has useful material on women and computing, women and management and women and technology generally. Some of the books used by women attending courses in the 19th and early 20th centuries on millinery, hairdressing and so on, may still be in the library but would need to be searched for in the main catalogue or the Rare Books Room. The archives include the Minutes of the Manchester Mechanics Institution, 1824 -1884; administrative records for various departments; student registers 1880s-1914 (with home addresses and occupation of father or sponsor); wages records; building plans; photographs; annual reports. These records are a fascinating source on women's education: it is possible for example to ascertain the proportion of male and female lecturers in various subjects, their salaries, length of service, grades etc.; the absence of women from certain posts and committees is often as revealing as their presence in other areas.

Union of Shop, Distributive and Allied Workers
Central Office
188 Wilmslow Road
Manchester M14 6LJ
Tel: 061 224 2804
Publications Officer: Mike Glover

Type of Institution: Trade Union Library serving as a repository for the records of the union and the organisations it developed from.

Access: By ringing in advance. The union is very helpful and welcoming to sympathetic researchers, but the library is also used as a meeting and interview room so it is not always possible to work there.

Catalogues: There is a separate series of author, title indexes for each cabinet of material.

Collections: Records of various shop workers unions with a large female membership; pamphlets, rule books etc.
Amalgamated Union of Cooperative Employers (AUCE) dating from the 1890s including Executive Council minutes; financial reports; conference material; journals (*The Co-operative Employee* 1910-20; *The Co-operative Official* 1919-1933).
National Amalgamated Union of Shop Assistants, Warehousemen and Clerks (NAUSA): annual reports 1891-1946; AGM agendas, minutes, 1917-1946; Executive Council minutes 1936-1946; General Secretary's reports 1936-46;
The Shop Assistant, a fascinating journal, 1896 -, which was published monthly until July 1901, then weekly, had a women's page which included fiction, biographies and autobiographies of members, union news (e.g. details of women's branches or councils, and work of women's organisers); discussions (e.g. January 1913 on 'why it is difficult to organise women'). The journal taken over by *Distributive Trades Journal* 1939.

National Union of Distributive and Allied Workers (NUDAW); Executive Committee minutes, 1921-46; membership lists; material relating to merger negotiations with NAUSA 1937 and 1947. *Distributive Trades Journal* 1939-1947 (taken over by *New Dawn*, established 1920, *NUDAW Journal* survives until 1973); this had a women's page which dealt with beauty, cookery etc.

USDAW: amalgamated union dates from 1947; Executive Council minutes, membership records; financial material; press cuttings 1950s Also miscellaneous local material dating back to the 1890s and the early 1900s: branch minute books; personal and organisation papers of officials etc. e.g. L. Lumley (AUCE organiser) and A Hewitt (Manchester and District Employees Association).

The library also holds much labour movement reference material: TUC reports; TUC Women's Advisory Committee material: Co-operative Union Congress reports: Labour Party material from 1905; General Federation of Trade Union material; Ministry of Labour's Labour Gazette, 1917-1968; Minutes of the War Emergency Workers National Committee 1914-1916. Small but good selection of early 20th century books on women and employment (eg Barbara Drake, *Women in the Engineering Trades*, 1917). Women's Industrial Council material: *Women's Wages in England in the 19th Century* (1906); *Women in Industry: A Bibliography* (1915); *The Manchester Sweated Industries Exhibition,* 1906 (includes descriptions of stalls).

Acts of Parliament, parliamentary papers and Department of Employment Equal Opportunities material are among the legal, general and parliamentary records.

Whitworth Art Gallery
Oxford Road
Manchester M15 6ER
Tel: 061-273 4865   Fax: 061-274 4543

Type of Institution: Founded at the turn of the century, now part of Manchester University. It has three primary collections -- Prints & Drawings, Textiles, and Wallpapers -- each with a small secondary library. The collections are detailed in *The First Hundred Years* (Whitworth 1989).

Access: Galleries open Monday - Saturday 10am - 5pm, Thursday to 9 pm. Prior appointments must be made with the department curators to use resources other than exhibitions on display, in study rooms. Normally appointments must be made on weekdays, although special appointments on Saturday may be available, subject to staffing.
Main galleries and toilets are wheelchair accessible, but study rooms are not.

Prints & Drawings Department
Curator Sarah Hyde

The British drawings and watercolours collection includes almost 70 women artists. Most of these are from the 19th century and 20th century although a few date from the 18th, beginning with Maria Cosway (1759-1838). The following artists are represented by more than two works: Edna Clarke-Hall (two illustrations for *Wuthering Heights)*, Kate Greenaway, Frances Hodgkins, Gwen John, Margaret Nicholls, Bridget Riley, Ethel Walker and Katerina Wilczynski. Four women sculptors are represented, including Barbara Hepworth. Forty-five women printmakers are represented, with numerous works of Mabel Annesley (7), Katherine Cameron (4), Suzanne Cooper (4), Joan Hassall (4), Gertrude Hermes (8), Clare Leighton (20), Mary Monkhouse (4),

Gwenda Morgan (17), Margaret Pilkington (25), Gwen Raverat (27), Lettice Sandford (11) and May Aimee Smith (19). The earliest are, again, Maria Cosway and Catherine-Maria Fanshawe, Mary Ann Hunter and Caroline Watson in the late 18th century and early 19th century. A list of works by women in each medium is available.

There are a few subject indices, which include portraits in painting, drawing and sculpture, but not in prints. There are many images of women in the collection, portrayed by artists of both sexes. Men's representations of women include a considerable collection of Pre-Raphaelite works. From a much earlier period, the print collection includes approximately 400 Dutch and Flemish prints of the 16th century and 17th century, some of which portray daily domestic life.

An exhibition *Women and Men,* in 1992, presented visitors with unlabelled pairs of works from the Gallery's collections and asked if they could tell which was by a woman and which by a man. Information from the exhibition can be consulted in the Print Room.

Textiles Department
Curator Jennifer Harris

The largest collection of flat textiles outside London, with over 11,000 pieces, including carpets, knitting, embroidery, printed fabrics, woven fabrics, lace, etc. All techniques are represented in the English collection, dating from the 16th century up to 20th century industrial fabrics, including many designed by women. Prior to the 20th century most textiles were created by women, the notable exception in England being weaving. For more information see the catalogue of the 1988 exhibition, 'Embroidery in women's lives 1300-1900', called *The Subversive Stitch* after Roszika Parker's 1984 book of the same title. The European collection includes silks, velvets, prints, embroidery and lace.

The Ethnographical collection has middle eastern tribal material - see for example the exhibition catalogue *The Qashqa'i of Iran* (1976) -- plus Greek, Turkish, Mediterranean and Coptic (Egyptian and Ethiopian) designs. Two late 4th century Coptic panels show female portraits of 'Autumn' and 'Winter'. It would be interesting to use the Egyptian textiles here in conjunction with the Egyptian artifacts in the Manchester Museum (see entry, above). There is also a video of women textile workers in West Africa, Stockport, India and China, a collection of handheld equipment, like needles, and examples of patchwork and quilting.

Wallpaper Department
Keeper Christine Woods

One of very few collections in the country, containing more than 3000 pieces. The original collection came to the Whitworth in 1967 from the industry collection of Wall Paper Manufacturers Ltd. Samples date from the 17th century to the present, but particular strengths are the last quarter of the 19th century (with a distinctly upmarket product), the first quarter of the 20th century (including papers aimed at the lower middle class), and the 1960s and 70s. The exhibition catalogue *A Decorative Art,* by Joanna Bannam (1985) shows the collection's Victorian wallpaper.

Women were involved in wallpaper in three ways: as designers, as producers and as consumers. Most wallpaper designers were anonymous; in the late 19th century and the 1960s, the two periods when designers were known by name, there were a few women, whose work is represented here. Kate Greenaway's drawings were incorporated into wallpaper, but not by her. In the production of wallpaper women did screenprinting, stencilling, and other jobs requiring cheap but dexterous labour, but they did not operate machinery. Among the uncatalogued photographs are pictures of workers and of wallpaper factories converted into munitions factories in World War II. Women were probably always the predominant purchasers of wallpaper. There are photographs of wallpaper showrooms in America around 1900 and in England in this century, showing female customers and male salesmen.

The female figure is a recurrent motif in wallpaper. The Whitworth's collection contains early 19th century examples such as the French panorama *Cupid and Psyche,* and has recently shown the portrayal of 'oriental' women in 20th century papers in a display featuring the use of Chinese and Japanese motifs in western surface pattern between the 18th century and the 20th century.

(Further examples of 18th century wallpapers may be found in Towneley Hall, the municipal gallery of Burnley, 25 miles north of Manchester and outside the scope of this guide. Tel: 0282-24213.)

Figure of Winter, Coptic c. late 4th century, courtesy of the Whitworth Art Gallery, University of Manchester.

149

Wigan Heritage Service
The History Shop,
Rodney Street,
Wigan WN1 1DG
Heritage Officer: 0942 828560

Since 1989 the Archives, Museums and Local History Services of Wigan Metropolitan Borough have been amalgamated into the Wigan Heritage Service which aims to preserve and interpret the heritage of the area to the broadest possible audience. The main public outlet is the 'History Shop' in Wigan town centre which also houses Wigan Local History Services; there is an Archives Office for the Borough, and a further Local History Library in Leigh. The Heritage Service produces a series of introductory leaflets on the various facilities and also has a regular newsletter, *Past Forward,* available free or on payment of a voluntary subscription (contact The Heritage Services Manager, Editor, 'Past Forward', Department of Leisure, Trencherfield Mill, Wigan WN3 4EF.) In addition to the archive and library services described below Wigan has extensive and various museum collections including Egyptology as well as local industrial and domestic materials. Permanent exhibitions are at the History Shop, Wigan Pier, Hindley Museum (at Hindley Library) and other sites, while recent temporary displays include 'a woman's place' which covered the domestic, political and employment history of local women (including pit-brow lasses). Further details about the museum holdings, and their accompanying documentation, can be obtained from the Heritage Officer.

Type of Institution: Archives Office holding the official records of the local authorities that formed the Metropolitan Borough of Wigan in 1974; a variety of organisational, family and personal papers; maps, photographs and a small reference library of printed books.

Access: Open, **by appointment only**, Monday, Tuesday, Thursday, Friday, 10 -1, 2 - 4.30. Documents are produced at 11.30 and 2.15. Archives Office is on the second floor of Leigh Town Hall; a lift gives disabled access.

Catalogues: There is a brief but very useful guide to the collections which can be supplemented by the more extensive lists in red folders. There are name, place and subject card indexes for the archives: the heading 'midwifery', for example, directs you to useful references in township records. The open shelf reference material is catalogued by author and subject, while name and street indexes are provided for the census records held on microfilm. A subject index, on cards, is a useful guide to the 'Miscellaneous Manuscript Portfolio' collection.

Collections:
Local Government material: is rich from the 17th century. For the ancient borough of Wigan there are Court Leet records from 1626, Court of Common Pleas records from 1618 (including cases of debt, slander and assault) and poor law material from the early 18th century. Typescript calendars, on open shelf, exist for the court records which contain many references to the activities of women in early modern Wigan. Miscellaneous material is available for the townships of Abram, Ashton, Atherton, Astley, Bedford, Haigh, Hindley, Ince, Pennington, Tyldesley and Westleigh: rate books, constables accounts, vestry minute

books, bastardy, apprenticeship and poor law material. Ince and Pennington have extensive workhouse, settlement, apprenticeship and bastardy records from the 18th century while Abram and Atherton's Poor Law papers date from 1698. There are typescript calendars for many of the series of pauper apprentice indentures - a source of evidence for the training and economic activities of women.

The 19th and 20th century local government records are voluminous: from 1835 there are minutes, accounts and correspondence for the Borough, later county Borough of Wigan. There are minutes, rate books and so on from the later 19th century, for thirteen Local Boards, later Urban District Councils: Abram, Ashton-in-Makerfield, Aspull, Atherton, Billinge, Golborne, Hindley, Ince, Leigh, Orrell, Pemberton, Standish and Tyldesley, and for the Rural District Councils of Leigh and Wigan. For Leigh Urban District (later a Borough Council) committee records include the minutes of the Maternity and Child Welfare Committee 1927 - 1948. Much local government material is not fully listed and is available with advance notice. For both Wigan and Leigh, there are complete minutes of the Boards of Guardians of the Poor from 1837.

Legal records: include Quarter Sessions material for Wigan from the 1730s, Coroners' records for the 19th and 20th centuries and mainly 20th century Petty Sessions material for Wigan and Leigh.

There are extensive **hospital records**, mainly concerning patients, for both Wigan and Leigh, 19th and 20th centuries.

Educational records include later 19th and 20th century local education authority material, and the records of many individual schools including Leigh Grammar School for Girls.

Church records cover over 30 Anglican parishes and some 70 nonconformist congregations, with Catholic material available on microfilm. The records of All Saints, Wigan date from the 17th century. Most church registers of baptisms, marriages and burials are shown only on microfilm at the History Shop.

Society and trade union records: include 20th century material for Wigan and District Weavers', Winders, Reelers and Beamers' Association; records of Ashton Evening Townswomen's Guild for the 1950s, a minute book for the Ladies Section of Wigan Swimming Club, 1922-9, and the records of the Wigan Vigilance Association, 1894-6.

Family papers: the Dicconson/Wrightington collection (D/D Wr) includes some early 19th colliery records and 19th century recipe books, but the Standish of Standish papers (D/D St) are probably the most promising for the history of women. They include a small book, 'Directions to make braids', kept by Cecilia Bindloss who married William Standish in 1660, with samples as well as instructions for different types of woven braid, and a notebook of the same period including recipes, songs and astrological calculations. From the later 17th century to the early 19th there is extensive correspondence from and concerning women members of the Standish family: the letters deal with health, household affairs, courtship, marital and parental relationships, including in this Catholic family, details of the progress of daughters as nuns in continental convents.

Solicitors' papers: are worth searching for material illustrating women's history: the papers of the Leigh firm Marsh, Son and Calvert (D/Dx Cal), include material on several 19th and 20th century women's estates as well as poor law and hospital material. Textiles, engineering and mining are represented among the **business records**: the papers of J and J Hayes, Leigh cotton spinners, date from the early 19th century and include a photograph album of 1900 portraying mill employees.

There is a variety of interesting material in the **artificial collections** (D/

Dz): the 'Pitmen's Strike Collection' from the 1840s, for example, has information on miners' wives. Two collections stand out. The aptly named 'Miscellaneous Manuscripts Portfolio' (D/Dz MMP) includes election material, posters and playbills, programmes for a variety of civic and royal celebrations - among them a programme for a demonstration and pageant at the Ritz Cinema, International Women's Day, 1944. The Edward Hall collection (D/Dz EHC) is an internationally important collection of diaries, with some correspondence and miscellaneous volumes, from the 17th to the 20th centuries. There are over forty **diaries** by women, many of them travel journals. Examples include Mrs Anna Walker's diaries from 1789 -1814 covering travel, domestic life and events in Europe during the Napoleonic Wars, and Dorothy Scholes' journal, kept during her service as a nursing sister in Exeter, 1914 -1918. The numerous male diaries also often have information on gender relationships and family life. A list of the diaries indicates which have been published and whether typescripts exist.

Wigan has one of the best local collections of **photographs** including over 1,000 photographs taken by William Wickham, Vicar of St Andrew's Wigan, mostly in the 1890s (see A.D. Gillies, *Wigan through Wickham's Window,* (1988)). Wickham took photographs of the church groups such as girls' classes and mothers' meetings, mill girls and pit-brow lasses, domestic and street scenes in Wigan, and a striking series of shots during the Wigan miners' strike of 1893. Information about photographs is also available in the local history libraries.

The Archives holds microfilms of the census, 1841 -1891, for the area covered by the post 1974 Metropolitan Borough. On open shelves there are some 20th century council minutes; publications of local record societies; reference works on local history and archives; local directories; typescripts and calendars of archive material and miscellaneous pamphlets covering aspects of the history of Wigan and the wider region.

Leigh Local History Service
Turnpike Centre (Leigh Library)
Civic Square,
Leigh WN7 1EB
Tel: 0942 604131

Type of Institution: Local history reference collection of printed items, maps, photographs and microform material mainly covering the area of the old Leigh Urban District and Borough Councils, located in the main Leigh library next to the Town Hall.

Access: Open: Monday, Tuesday, Thursday, Friday, 10.am - 7.pm; Wednesday 10.am -5.pm; Saturday 10.am - 3.30pm. Researchers needing to use microform material should book in advance; as should those with specialist inquiries as the local history officer may not always be available. Disabled access good.

Catalogues: There are two main card indexes, one for Leigh and one for Lancashire; both include authors, titles, and subjects. There are indexes to the *Leigh Chronicle* and the *Leigh Journal* and indexes to census returns and parish registers are available on request.

Collections: There are several thousand **printed books** on the history of Leigh, Wigan and the surrounding region; local history periodicals, theses on local topics, pamphlets and news-cuttings. Printed minutes, annual reports and leaflets of local organisations, hospitals, Poor Law Guardians etc are often useful sources while the publications of Local Authorities are also kept. There are full holdings of local newspapers, including the *Leigh Advertiser* from 1848, and the *Leigh Chronicle* from 1852. Most newspapers are available in microform as are parish registers, and census returns (1841-1891). Maps and photographs concerning the Leigh area of the Metropolitan Borough are also here. Some material is on open shelf; most has to be requested at the Local History Enquiry Desk.

Wigan Local History Service
The History Shop
Rodney Street,
Wigan WN1 1DG
Tel: 0942 82020

Type of Institution: Local history reference collection for the Metropolitan Borough of Wigan; it holds similar material to that at Leigh, but with more comprehensive coverage of the whole of the present authority. It is housed in the old Wigan Library, designed by Alfred Waterhouse and built in 1878, which has recently been reopened as the headquarters of Wigan Heritage Services. The 'History Shop' contains a permanent exhibition on the history of Wigan, space for temporary exhibitions, a meeting room and a shop selling local history publications and souvenirs, as well as a Research Centre.

Access: Open: Monday, 10.am -7.pm; Tuesday - Friday, 10am - 5pm; Saturday, 10.am -1.pm. Microform readers must be booked in advance. No disabled access.

Catalogues: There is a subject index to the Local History Collection; a biographical index; subject indexes to the local and newspaper cuttings collections; indexes to the *Colliery Guardian,* and the *Wigan Observer* (to 1900); and indexes to Census returns. Most references under 'women' are to work.

Collections: There are useful items on local women's history amongst the printed books and articles: the subject index, under 'coal and coal mining', for example, directs you to Angela John's articles and book, *By the Sweat of Their Brow* (1980) on Wigan 'pit-brow lasses'. Open shelf material includes local history books, historical and genealogical reference works; the publications of local record societies and printed local

156

government minutes. Pamphlets, conference proceedings, reports and minutes of a variety of local organisations and public bodies are available on request. Wigan **newspapers** from the 1820s can be consulted in **microform**, as can parish registers (including Catholic and non-conformist material), census returns, and hearth tax records. Much local archive material has been microfilmed for consultation at Wigan. Copies of **photographs** are arranged in a series of folders by place or topic ('royal visits', 'walking days', etc). Folder 11 covers pictures of 'Warship Week', 1941, and includes the marches on 'Women's Day' of women munitions workers, and women in the voluntary and military services.

Working Class Movement Library
51 The Crescent
Salford M5 4WX
Tel: 061 736 3601
Librarian: Alain Kahan

Type of Institution: The library was originally compiled by Ruth and Edmund Frow over a period of many years and housed at their home in Old Trafford, Manchester, where it attracted considerable renown and many visitors. It moved to its present site opposite Salford University on a building provided by Salford City Council, with full-time staff in 1987. It is a magnificent collection of c.16,000 books, c.15,000 pamphlets, and organisational records, which is now a mecca for all researchers interested in the history of socialism, early radicalism, the labour movement and 'working people'. For historians of women, there is a wealth of material buried in pamphlets, journals, biographies, trade union records and various kinds of printed sources. In addition there is a good collection of banners, photographs and other ephemera of the socialist, labour and trade union movements, with many items of interest to historians of women. We have selected examples which give some indication of what researchers might find, but the list is certainly not exhaustive.

Access: Opening hours are Tuesday, Wednesday, Friday 10am -5pm; Thursday 10am -7pm; alternate Sundays 2pm -5pm; disabled access via ramp at rear; photocopying available. The Library can be reached by train from Preston and Manchester to Salford Crescent station; by buses numbers 66, 67, 68 to Salford Crescent and by car on the A6.

Catalogue: There is a card catalogue arranged by author, title, subject and classification number (a modified version of the Dewey system). Unless you have specific items in mind, the heading 'women' in the subject catalogue is a useful place to start as it includes numerous subheadings such as 'engineering', 'political parties', 'industrial labour', 'legal status', 'world wars 1 and 2', 'social roles and functions', 'suffrage', 'women's movement'. However, much of the original collection is still being catalogued and the Library is constantly expanding. For material such as trade union records, journal articles, and pamphlets it is necessary to be enterprising and creative in your search. The Library produces a regular *Bulletin* with short articles about the collections. Furthermore, the Frows' own publications (such as *Political Women 1800 -1850* and *The 'Half-time' System in Education*) are usually compiled from the Library's material and so give some indication of holdings.

Collections: We have arranged the following examples partly by theme, and partly by type of material. All items should be ordered from the catalogue; staff will bring it to be consulted in the Reading Room.

Printed books: There are rich 19th century holdings covering the early radical movement, Chartism and political and social reform. They include some relatively unknown works by and about women, as well as more familiar items: Mary Ann Radcliffe, *The Female Advocate; or an attempt to recover the Rights of Women from Male Usurpation (1799);* Priscilla Wakefield, *Reflections on the Present Condition of the Female Sex; with suggestions for its improvement* (1817); *Suppressed Defence. The defence of Mary Anne Carlisle, to the Vice Society's Indictment Against the Appendix to the Theological Works of Thomas Paine* (1821); William Thompson, *Appeal of One Half of the Human Race, Women, Against the Pretensions of Mr Mill's Celebrated 'Article on Government'* (1825); Frances Morrison, *Lecture on Marriage and Women* (1838); John Parker *Women's Mission* (1840); Mrs John Sandford, *Woman in her Social and Domestic Charter* (1842); Mrs Jameson, *Sisters of Charity and the Commission of Labour* (1859); J. Watkins, *Address to the Women of England* (n.d.). There are books on Mary Wollstonecraft and works by Harriet Martineau. Illustrations of women's lives and work are found in Henry Brown, *The Cotton Fields and Cotton Factories* (early 19th century), *The Book of Trades,* vols 1-3 (1811), *The Useful Arts and Manufactures of Great Britain* (1848). Advice to working-class women is given in *The Working Man's Wife by* the *'Author of the Family Book' (1844)* while *Lancashire Homes, and What Ails Them* (1863) shows middle-class perceptions of working-class lives at home and in paid employment.

From the later 19th and 20th century there are many essays, histories, biographies and auto-biographies. There is an excellent collection of books by and about women from the late 19th century, particularly strong on women's movements, working conditions, and biographical material. These are a selection: Mrs S.A. Sewell, *Women and the Times We Live In* (Manchester, 1869); John Duguid Milne, *Industrial Employment of Women of the Middle and Lower Ranks* (1870); Mrs Ashton Dilke, *Women's Suffrage* (c.1880); Clementina Black, *A Working Woman's Speech from the 19th Century* (1889); Ada Heather-Bigg, *Women and the Glove Trade* (1891); Allen C. Clarke, *Effects of the Factory System on Women and Children* (Bolton, 1899); Helen Blackburn, *Women's Suffrage: A Record of the Woman's Suffrage Movement in the British Isles* - includes material on Lydia Becker (1902); Josephine Goldmark, *Labour Laws for Women in the U.S.A.* (1904); Constance Williams, *How Women Can Help in Political Work: Practical Hints on Local Organisation and Electioneering* (1905); Evelyn Sharp, *Rebel Women* (1910); Charlotte Despard, *Women in the New Era* (1910); Eleanor Rathbone, *The Problem of Women's Wages* (1912); H.F. Normanton, *Sex Differentiation in Salary* (n.d., c. 1914); Millicent Malleson, *A Woman Doctor, Mary Murdoch of Hull* (1919); Marguerite Bennet, *Wanted Womanhood, Charlotte Cowdray (*the life of a woman teacher, 1864 -1932*);* Sylvia Anthony, *Women's Place in Industry and the Home* (1932); Joan Beauchamp, *Women Who Work* (1937) - includes useful statistics; S. Wyatt, *Absenteeism among Women* (1943) and *Women on War Work* (1945); Nan Berger and Joan Maizels, *Women -Fancy or Free? Some Thoughts on Woman's Status in Britain Today* (1962).

There are numerous biographies or autobiographies of prominent and politically active women: *Elizabeth Ham by Herself* (1785 -1820); Memoirs and Correspondence of Hannah More; Angelica Bababanoff,

My Life as a Rebel (1938) - an account of the socialist movement in Italy and Russia are examples.

The Library also includes works by lesser-known novelists, such as Margaret Harkness, *A City Girl* and *A Manchester Shirtmaker;* and Ethel Holdsworth Carnie, a Lancashire mill-worker from age 11 who produced poetry and prose for many socialist and women's journals in the early 20th century. Works by Carnie here include, *Songs of a Factory Girl; Rhymes from the Factory; Voices of Womanhood;* and novels such as *This Slavery, Miss Nobody, General Belinda.*

Journals: There is a good range of 19th and 20th century radical, socialist and labour movement material including original and reprint journals and newspapers.

Women's Journals include: *The Englishwoman's Review* (1870-72); Annie Besant, ed, *Our Corner* (1883, 1886, 1888); a complete run of *The Woman Worker* (1907- 9, and 1911-) with a run of *Women Folk* as it was called in 1910; *The Common Cause* (1909-1910); *Votes for Women* (1911-12).

Journals with important contributions by women include *The People's Journal* (1847-8) for which Harriet Martineau and other women wrote; *Meliora* (1861-9) - a social sciences journal; *Social Notes Concerning Social Reformers, Social Requirements, Social Progress (*1878-80) with articles on 'The Ladies' Sanitary Association'.

Radical and Socialist Journals: *New Moral World* (1834 -1845); *Justice* (1888-1900) - journal of the Social Democratic Federation; *The Social Democrat* (1897 -1911); *The Clarion; The Young Socialist* (1907 -22, incomplete); *The British Socialist* (1912-13); *Labour Leader* (1916, 1939-70); *The Red Dawn* (1919-20) which had a women's column; *The Plebs* - journal of the National Council of Labour Colleges with occasional articles by women such as Ellen Wilkinson; *The Communist* (1920-1940, incomplete); *The Daily Worker* (1942 -present day); *The New Propellor* (1935-47) - put out by the Aircraft Shop Stewards National Council, includes information on women in engineering during the second world war. Cooperative Society Journals include: *Woman's Outlook* (1925-62, incomplete); *Millgate Monthly* (c.1900 - 1940); *Scottish Cooperator* (1901-43, incomplete) contains information on the Scottish Cooperative Women's Guild.

Pamphlets: There are extensive collections with much of interest in files besides those marked 'women'. The following subject areas are covered: trades councils; trades unions; Trade Union Congress Women's Conferences (1940-83); Labour Party Women's Conferences (1963 -74); Labour Party; Independent Labour Party; Social Democratic Federation; British Socialist Party; Communist Party; Labour Research Department; Peace and No Conscription Fellowship (with material of the Women's International League for Peace and Freedom); Women's Freedom League; Union for Democratic Control; Women under Fascism; Fabian Tracts; the Webbs; the Spanish Civil War (including material on nurses); education; birth control (including Annie Besant and Marie Stopes); suffrage; Open Door Council; temperance; Women Workers; Alexandra Kollontai; Maude Royden.

The following are more detailed examples of especial interest.
Feminist organisations and individuals:
The International Congress of Women, *Report of Council Transactions,* ed. Countess of Aberdeen (1899), with other volumes of this body, the forerunner of the National Union of Women Workers, later the National Council of Women. National Union of Women's Suffrage Societies, Annual Reports, 1911-14, 1916-17; National Union of Women's Suffrage Societies, North Hertfordshire Society, Annual Reports, 1909-19. Mary Philips, *The Militant Suffrage Campaign in Perspective* (n.d., Suffrage Fellowship); *They Couldn't Stop Us* (n.d.) - on suffragette imprisonment; Christabel Pankhurst, *Industrial Salvation* (1918). W. Lyon Blease, *Against Prejudice* (Women's Freedom League). National League for Opposing Women's Suffrage, pamphlet opposing women M.P.s (n.d.). National Union of Societies for Equal Citizenship, Annual Reports, 1918-1930; National Council for Equal Citizenship, Annual Reports, 1932-3, 1935-38; NUSEC, *Equal Pay for Equal Work* (1927).

Open Door Council Publications, c. 1920-1930 including *Statutory and Trade Union Restrictions on the Employment of Women* (c 1925). Six Point Group, *The Protection of Industrial Women*. Chrystal MacMillan, *The Nationality of Married Women* (1931). Emma Goldman, *The Traffic in Women and Other Essays on Feminism*. National Committee for the Celebration of International Women's Day, *Women on the March*, 1943. International Women's Year Celebrations, 1975-6; and much recent feminist material.

Women and employment: examples include: Women's Industrial Council, *Women as Barmaids* (1905); Elaine Burton, *Domestic Work, Britain's Largest Industry* (1943); Herbert Fox, *Woven from a Stone*, the story of the Quantock Weavers; Industrial Welfare Society, *Welfare for Women and Girls*, n.d.; Mary Macarthur Holiday Homes for Working Women, Annual Report, 1972-3.

Women and social reform: W.T. Stead, speech in court, 1885. Maternal Mortality Committee, London, 1918 material. *The Woman's View*, (Women's True Temperance Committee, 1933). *Prison for Women* (Life in Holloway, 1943)

Material on peace and war: Women's International League for Peace and Freedom, Manchester Branch, *Annual Report,* 1931. Parliament of Women, Report of the First Session, 1941; Address at the West Riding Women's Parliament, 1941; Report of the second session, and *Health and Housing*, Report of the 4th session of the London Women's Parliament, 1940s. (The Parliament of Women was a non-party organisation which brought together Trade Unions, Women's Cooperative Guilds, housewives' groups, Communist Party women and professional associations to coordinate women's part in the war effort, and to prepare future policies). Other second World War material includes the pamphlets, *Home Front* and Betty Sinclair, *Ulster Women and the War* There is much historical and contemporary material on the peace movement, with a good selection of books and other material on conscientious objectors; the British Peace Committee; the British

Section of Medical Aid for Vietnam; Campaign for Nuclear Disarmament (national and local material); the early days of the Committee of 100; and the Greenham Common Women's Peace Camp.

Political Party Material:
ILP and Labour Party: Salford City Labour Party Minute Books, 1920 - 1975, including Radcliffe Women's Section Minutes, 1934 - 46; full run of Labour Party Annual Reports from 1901; Labour Party Year Book; pamphlets and reports of the Independent Labour Party, 1893 - 1935; publications of the Standing Joint Committee of Industrial Women's Organisations (Advisory Committee to the Labour Party) including, *Report on Equal Pay for Equal Work* (c. 1925) and *First Steps towards a Domestic Workers' Charter* (1933); leaflets of the Women's Labour League.

Communist Party of Great Britain: various pamphlets about women e.g. *Work among Women* (1924); newsletters etc; *Women Today,* Communist Party women's paper, for 1944 and other years; manuscript lecture notes for a Communist Party school for women cadres, Heysham, 1955. There are also miscellaneous items concerning women from the Communist Party of Ireland.

Miscellaneous political material: Socialist Women of Greater New York, *Olive Johnson. Woman and the Socialist Movement* (1908); Clara Zetkin, *Lenin on the Woman Question* (1934); Hilda Browning, *Women under Fascism and Communism; Fascist War on Women,* 1930s pamphlet on Italian women political prisoners.

Irish collections: There is extensive material on Ireland including biographies of Mary Ann McCracken, Maud Gonne and Constance Markieviez.

Trade union records:
There is a good selection of printed books on the trade union movement and on the local history of Greater Manchester.
The following is a selection of other material held: General and Municipal Workers Union, later the General, Municipal and Boilermak-

ers' Union, (1904-1987, incomplete): minutes, annual reports, reports of the annual congress, plus unions's *Journal* (1920-84, incomplete). National Union of Tailors and Garment Workers: minutes, circulars, journals, reports (1868 -1931); Amalgamated Union of Clothiers Operatives, (1900-14); Amalgamated Society of Tailors and Tailoresses: rare ephemera of this largely East End of London Jewish Union. Amongst extensive other material relating to textile unions are the Reports of the United Textile Factory Workers Association (1909 - 1973) which had many women members. National Union of Clerks: *Journal* (1908 -50) and minute books of local branches; Association of Women Clerks and Secretaries - photographs and news-clippings. Amalgamated Engineering Union, District Committee Minutes (1915 - 1986); women were admitted to this union in 1945. Reports of the General Federation of Trade Unions (1899-1985, incomplete): the National Federation of Women Workers and other Unions sent women as delegates.

International Trade Unions' Women's Conference, Proceedings, 1927. Manchester and Salford Trades Council - Conference on the organisation of women workers; Manchester and Salford Women's Trade Union Council, *Annual Reports*, (1900, 1902 -4, 1912-17).

Women Must Organise - pamphlet from 1932. Trades Union Congress - full run of reports of annual Congress, 1878 - ; T.U.C. Women Workers' Annual Conference, Reports, 1940-83, incomplete; includes TUC's *Charter for Women at Work*. International Trade Union Women's Conference, 1927: Addresses and Proceedings. National Society of Woolcombers and Kindred Trades, Report on the Employment of Women on night-shift (1916); USDAW, *Rights for Working Women* (1975); NALGO, *Report of the Equal Rights Working Party* (1975).

Photographs: The wide-ranging collection includes women workers, Clarion, trade union and peace demonstrations.

Thesis: the library has a copy of Carol Edyth Morgan, *Working Class Women and Labor and Social Movements of mid-19th Century England* (University of Iowa D.Phil, 1979).

Appendix One

Theses

The following is a list of some of the most useful recent theses on women's studies produced for degrees at higher education institutions in Manchester. They are available on inter-library loan or for consultation in the library of the relevant Universities. Of course, more theses will have been completed by the time this *Guide* is published.

Manchester University
Education Theses:
Joyce Goodman, 'Women and the management of the Education of Working Class Girls, 1800 -1861', (Ph.D, 1992).
Joan Hassall, 'The Bennett Street Sunday School, Manchester. A study in 19th century education and social improvement', (Ph.D, 1986).
John Kehoe, 'The Secular Activities of Sunday Schools in Manchester and Salford in the 19th century', (M.Ed, 1985).
Sheila Lemoine, 'The North of England Council for Promoting the Higher Education of Women, 1867 -1875-6', (M.Ed., 1968).
Marie Pointon, 'The Growth of Women's Sport in late Victorian Society as Reflected in Contemporary Literature', (M.Ed., 1978).
Frederick Pugh, 'Childhood and Youth in Late 19th Century Manchester, with particular reference to the Boys' and Girls' Welfare Society, 1870 -1900', (M.Ed., 1980).

Government Theses:
Karen Hunt, 'Equivocal Feminists: The Social Democratic Federation and the Woman Question', (Ph.D, 1988).
Joni Lovenduski, 'Rosa Luxembourg and the Working Class Party (the SPD) in Germany, 1900 -1919', (M.A., 1976).

History Theses:

Helen Boak, 'The Status of Women in the Weimar Republic', (Ph.D, 1982).

Clare Evans, 'The Separation of Work and Home? The Case of the Lancashire Textiles 1825 -1865', (Ph.D, 1991).

Judith Fincher, 'The Clarion Movement' (M.A., 1971).

Patricia Higgins, 'Women in the English Civil War,' (M.A., 1965).

Angela John, 'Women Workers in British Coal Mines, 1840 -1890, with special reference to West Lancashire', (Ph.D, 1976).

Janet Lambertz, 'The Politics and Economics of Family Violence, from the Late 19th century to 1948', (M.Phil, 1984).

Linda Walker, 'The Women's Movement in England in the Late 19th and Early 20th centuries', (Ph.D, 1984).

The following theses were produced as part of an M.A. course in late Victorian and Edwardian Society:

Margaret Beetham, 'Education and Social Welfare in late 19th century Manchester with special reference to the work of the Manchester School Board' (1974).

Susan Bryan, 'Women's Suffrage in the Manchester Area, c. 1890 - 1906' (1977).

Karen Hunt, 'An Examination of the Burnley Social Democratic Federation' (1979).

Miriam Steiner, 'Philanthropic Activity and Organisation in the Manchester Jewish Community 1867 -1914' (1974).

Linda Walker, 'The Employment Question and the Women's Movement in late Victorian and Edwardian Society with Particular Reference to "The Englishwoman's Review"' (1974).

Sociology Theses

Susan Edwards, 'Female Sexuality, the Law and Society: changing socio-legal conceptions of the rape victim in Britain since 1800', (Ph.D, 1979).

Catherine Emmet Leech, 'The Feminist Movement in Manchester 1903 -1914', (M.A., 1971).

Iris Miner, 'Ideology and the Sociology of the Working Class Family, 1870 -1914', (Ph.D, 1986).

Peter Rushton, 'Housing Conditions and the Family Economy in the Victorian Slum: a study of a Manchester district [Ancoats], 1790 - 1871', (Ph.D, 1977).

Patricia Thornhill, 'The State Evacuation Scheme, 1939-40, Manchester', (M.A., 1982).

Manchester Metropolitan University
(previously Manchester Polytechnic)

The following are amongst many useful theses produced as part of the M.A. in the history of the Manchester region.

Wendy Foulger, 'Work and Gender, Ideology in the Lancashire Cotton Industry, 1910-1920', (1988).

Catharine Rew, 'Jewish Women and Philanthropy in Manchester, 1884 -1914, with particular reference to the Jewish Ladies Visiting Association', (1989).

Books on Manchester Women's History

This is a selective bibliography for those interested in the history of women in Manchester. We are grateful to the staff at Tameside Local History Library, whose *Tameside Bibliography* has been very useful in compiling the list.

Rickie Burman, 'The Jewish woman as breadwinner: the changing value of women's work in a Manchester immigrant comunity', *Oral History*, 10 (1982)

Burman, 'Growing up in Manchester Jewry - the Story of Clara Weingard,' *Oral History Journal* 12 (1984)

Burman, 'Jewish Women and the Household Economy in Manchester, c. 1890 -1920', in David Cesarini, ed, *The Making of Modern Anglo-Jewry* (1990)

J.A.V. Chapple, *Elizabeth Gaskell: a portrait in letters* (1980)

Andrew Davies, *Leisure, Gender and Poverty: Working Class Culture in Salford and Manchester, 1900-1939* (1992)

Andrew Davies and Steven Fielding, *Workers Worlds: Culture and Communities in Manchester and Salford 1880 -1939* (1992) for M. Tebbutt on 'Gossip and Women's Words'; and Ann Hughes and Karen Hunt, '"A Culture transformed?"': Women's Lives in Wythenshawe in the 1930s'.

Clare Evans, 'Unemployment and the making of the feminine during the Lancashire Cotton Famine', in Pat Hudson and W.R. Lee, eds, *Women's Work and the family economy in historical perspective* (1990)

Edmund and Ruth Frow, eds, *Political Women 1800-1850* (1989)

Winifred Gerin, *Elizabeth Gaskell: a biography* (1976)

Sheila Goodie, *Annie Horniman: a pioneer in the theatre (1990)*

Edward Higgs, *Domestic Servants and Households in Rochdale 1851-1911* (1986)

Mary Kingsland Higgs, *Mary Higgs of Oldham* (1954)

Patricia Hollis, *Ladies Elect: Women in English Local Government 1865 -1914* (1987)

Angela John, *By the Sweat of their Brow. Women Workers at Victorian Coal Mines (1984)*.

Angela John, ed, *Unequal Opportunities: Women's Employment in England 1800 -1918* (1986) for Higgs on Rochdale, and some useful general material.

Jan Lambertz, 'Sexual Harrassment in the 19th century English Cotton Industry' *History Workshop*, 19 (Spring 1985)

Gifford Lewis, *Eva Gore Booth and Esther Roper. a biography* (1988)

Jane Lewis, ed, *Labour and Love: Women's Experience of home and family life 1850 -1940* (1986) a useful collection with some references to the North West.

Jill Liddington, and Jill Norris, *One Hand Tied Behind Us* (1978)

Jane Rendall,ed, *Equal or Different? Women's Politics 1800-1914* (1987) - essays with some references to the North West.

Barbara Taylor, *Eve and the New Jerusalem: socialism and feminism in the 19th century* (1983)

Melanie Tebbutt, *Making Ends Meet: Pawnbroking and working class credit* (1983)

Betty Vernon, *Ellen Wilkinson* (1982)

There are two particularly useful journals: *North West Labour History* (previously *Bulletin of the North West Society for the Study of Labour History*) has had two special issues on women, vol 7 (1980-81) and vol. 12 (1987). The first included Karen Hunt on women and the Social Democratic Federation in Bolton and Jill Liddington on Selina Cooper; the second, Joyce Whitehead on Alice Foley, Mary Kirrane on women office workers, and Manchester Women's History Group on women and housing.

Manchester Region History Review has regular articles on local libraries, record offices and museums along with frequent articles on women's history, including:

Kate Rigby, 'Annot Robinson, A Forgotten Manchester Suffragette' (vol 1, 1, Spring 1987); Joan Parker, 'Lydia Becker. Pioneer Orator' (vol 5, 2, 1991-2); Melanie Tebbutt, 'Public and Private Space' (vol 6, 1992).

Source Material:

Clementina Black, *Married Women's Work* (Virago reprint 1983)
Ada Nield Chew, *The Life and Writings of a Working Woman* (Virago reprint, 1982)
Katherine Chorley, *Manchester Made Them* (1950) -middle class life before the first World War.
Stella Davies, *North Country Bred* (1963 and later editions)
Alice Foley, *A Bolton Childhood* (1973)
Alice Lock, ed, *Looking Back at Stalybridge* (1989)
Hannah Mitchell, *The Hard Way Up* (Virago reprint, 1977)
Sylvia Pankhurst, *The Suffragette Movement* (Virago reprint, 1977)
Elizabeth Raffald, *Directory Of Manchester and Salford* (first published 1772, reprinted by Neil Richardson, Swinton)
Robert Roberts, *The Classic Slum* (1971 and later editions)
Mary Stocks, *My Commonplace Book* (1970).

The early 20th century classic, *Life as we have known it by Co-operative Working Women,* ed, Margaret Llewellyn Davies (Virago reprint, 1977) includes the account of a Stockport, 'Felt Hat Worker' as well as Oldham and Manchester material. *Maternity. Letters from Working Women* (Virago, 1978) is useful though less locally specific.

Many recent autobiographies are being published by local history or adult education groups: Mary Bentley, *Born 1896. Childhood in Clayton and Working in Manchester and Cheshire* (1985); Mavis Sapple, *A Salford Childhood* (1984); Lilian Slater, *'Think On', said Mam. Life in Bradford, Manchester 1911- 1919* (1984) are examples.

M. Barrow, *Women, 1870-1928: A Select Guide to Printed and Archival Sources in the United Kingdom* (1981) has a broader geographic scope, but a narrower thematic and chronological span than this present guide; it may offer additional avenues for those researching the 19th and 20th centuries. (A copy can be consulted in the Archives Department of Manchester Central Library).

Other Places of Interest

Although we have tried to include as many institutions as possible in our guide, unfortunately we have not been able to visit every library, museum and art gallery in Greater Manchester. The following will also be of interest to researchers:

Heywood Central Library
Church Street, Heywood. Tel: 0706 60947.

Middleton Central Library
Long Street, Middleton. Tel: 061 643 5228.
Middleton, now part of Rochdale, is one of the oldest mill towns in the region. The local history library has the Samuel Bamford Collection, material about Lady Susan Hopwood - an active 'clean air' campaigner at the turn of the century, a good collection of photographs and a well-referenced newspaper index.

Museum of Transport
Boyle Street, Manchester 8. Tel: 061 205 2122.
The collection includes some sixty historic vehicles which represent almost one hundred years of local road transport history. The archives which are available to researchers by prior arrangement, include photographs and items which illustrate aspects of local passenger transport.

Ordsall Hall Museum
Taylorson Street, Salford M5 3EX. Tel: 061 872 0251.
This is part of Salford Museums and Art Gallery Service.

Pankhurst Centre
60-62 Nelson Street, Manchester M13 9WP. Tel: 061 273 5673.
This is the former home of Emmeline Pankhurst, now restored by the Pankhurst Trust to commemorate the suffrage movement; it is used as an exhibition centre and meeting place for community and women's groups.

Index

Shortage of space has made it impossible to list all individuals, organisations and industries separately. Places named only as part of a current local authority have not been separately indexed. Researchers should check general headings such as trade unions, women artists, employment.